W9-AQM-806

# PETER SHAFFER

CASEBOOKS ON MODERN DRAMATISTS
(VOL. 10)

GARLAND REFERENCE LIBRARY
OF THE HUMANITIES
(VOL. 1291)

# CASEBOOKS ON MODERN DRAMATISTS
## (*General Editor*, Kimball King)

# PETER SHAFFER
## *A Casebook*

C.J. Gianakaris

GARLAND PUBLISHING, INC. • NEW YORK & LONDON
1991

**Library of Congress Cataloging-in-Publication Data**

Peter Shaffer : a casebook / [edited by] C.J. Gianakaris.
    p. cm. — (Garland reference library of the humanities ; vol.
1291. Casebooks on modern dramatists ; vol. 10)
    Includes bibliographical references (p.   ) and index.
    ISBN 0–8240–6889–0
    1. Shaffer, Peter, 1926–   Criticism and interpretation.
I. Gianakaris, C.J., 1934–  . II. Series: Garland reference
library of the humanities ; vol. 1291. III. Series: Garland
reference library of the humanities. Casebooks on modern dramatists ;
vol. 10.
PR6037.H23Z79   1991
822'.914—dc20                        91–18449
                                        CIP

Printed on acid-free, 250-year-life paper
Manufactured in the United States of America

# CONTENTS

# GENERAL EDITOR'S NOTE

For the tenth volume in Garland's *Casebooks on Modern Dramatists*, C. J. Gianakaris, professor of English at Western Michigan University, has collected a series of essays on the British playwright Peter Shaffer. Gianakaris has recently completed a book-length study of the playwright, entitled *Peter Shaffer*, published by Macmillan in the United Kingdom. He is the author of many articles on contemporary dramatists and half a dozen books, including *Foundations of the Drama* in 1975. A co-founder of *Comparative Drama*, Gianakaris has the wide-ranging knowledge of authors and trends in the modern theatre that makes his placement of Shaffer in the forefront of contemporary dramatists authoritative. Shaffer's popularity, analyses of his best-known plays and insights into his themes and techniques are related here in detail.

Kimball King

# PREFACE

## C. J. Gianakaris

Eleven articles make up the following collection centered on the highly successful British playwright Peter Shaffer. Born in 1926, Shaffer came to the theater gradually after writing broadcast dramas for radio and television as well as several mystery novels. But it is the dramatist's major pieces written for the legitimate stage—from *Five Finger Exercise* forward—which receive primary attention here.

"The Artistic Trajectory of Peter Shaffer" opens the book with an overview of the playwright's career, artistically and commercially. Notwithstanding impressive success in both the subsidized theaters in England and the commercial venues of the West End and Broadway, Peter Shaffer inspires contradictory responses from drama critics—an anomaly addressed in the lead essay. A rare sampling of Peter Shaffer's own thoughts, directly expressed, emerges in "A Conversation with Peter Shaffer (1990)." He comments informally there on his recent comedy *Lettice & Lovage*, society today, and the theater in general to share the thoughts on his mind at this moment in his life.

Charles R. Lyons follows with a penetrating look at *Five Finger Exercise*. Lyons in "Peter Shaffer's *Five Finger Exercise* and the Conventions of Realism" examines the mostly weakened conventions of dramatic realism Shaffer utilized in his earliest hit play, pointing out that the playwright quickly abandoned that idiom to develop more eclectic theatrical responses during the following decades of his flourishing career. Gene A. Plunka is concerned with several of Shaffer's early stage works in "'Know Thyself': Integrity and Self-Awareness in the Early Plays of Peter Shaffer." He believes that the dialectic found in Shaffer's later major dramas—the conflict between

*ix*

individual freedom and structured institutionalized mores—already is present in the early pieces. Meanwhile, by surveying many of Shaffer's plays, Barbara Lounsberry seeks to trace the dramatist's evolving metaphysical position. In her essay entitled "The Cosmic Embrace: Peter Shaffer's Metaphysics," Professor Lounsberry focuses on Shaffer's persistent concern for answers to philosphical and metaphysical questions involving being, identity, freedom, and especially the divine. James R. Stacy's trail-blazing study from the mid-seventies, "The Sun and the Horse: Peter Shaffer's Search for Worship," is reprinted next. Stacy effectively isolates the quest for worship that dominated Shaffer's first major successes (namely, *The Royal Hunt of the Sun* and *Equus*), noting that Shaffer ends up discounting conventional religions because they are too restrictive to permit full actualization of "the multiplicity of self, which demands a multiplicity of gods."

Peter Shaffer's best known play to date is the extraordinarily successful *Amadeus*, a work that earned the writer a Tony Award and, in its movie incarnation, an Oscar. Three essays in this volume are devoted to the rich fabric of *Amadeus*. Felicia Hardison Londré in "Straddling a Dual Poetics in *Amadeus*: Salieri as Tragic Hero and Joker" lends a provocative, fresh perspective to the drama. By considering the chief protagonist a combined tragic hero and joker figure, Professor Londré suggests that Shaffer embraced two very different, even opposed, poetic systems, thereby to win Salieri sympathy but also sardonic laughter. A viewpoint on the issue of historical authenticity in *Amadeus* is found in my earlier discussion "Fair Play? Peter Shaffer's Treatment of Mozart in *Amadeus*" reprinted from *Opera News*.

Shaffer's more recent dramas are the subject of the final two essays in this collection. Dennis A. Klein focuses on a repeated motif in the playwright's works, the playing of games by the play's protagonists. In "Game-Playing in Four Plays by Peter Shaffer: *Shrivings, Equus, Lettice and Lovage*, and *Yonadab*," Klein assembles the games that arise in these dramas to constitute a pattern underlying Shaffer's works, both early and late. Michael Hinden, meanwhile, in "'Where All the Ladders Start': The Autobiographical Impulse in Shaffer's Recent Work" ingeniously pursues a biographical approach originally commenced earlier by the psychiatrist-scholar Jules Glenn. Hinden's thoughtful discussion moves beyond Glenn's early studies, however, to discern patterns of twinship even in Shaffer's most recent writing.

Toward the end of the book stand three useful sections. "Contributors" offers affiliation identifications for the writers of the essays; "Play Openings" assembles a basic chronology for Shaffer's stage works; and "Selected Bibliography" lists the most crucial published criticism of Shaffer. Finally, the editor and essayists intend through this book to make Peter Shaffer a more familiar figure both to general and specialized readers. These provocative discussions should provide valuable insights into the art of a foremost dramatist of our time, Peter Shaffer.

# Peter Shaffer

# THE ARTISTIC TRAJECTORY OF PETER SHAFFER

## C. J. Gianakaris

British playwright Peter Shaffer remains a puzzle today, particularly for critics and academic scholars. A "moving target" with respect to dramatic styles and thematic interests, he is difficult to categorize within tidy literary designations. Is he primarily a realist probing the psychological and social issues facing the modern age? Is he a somber metaphysician seeking answers to universal enigmas? Or is he a teasing farceur who targets mundane human follies? Regular theatergoers will recognize elements of all these types in Shaffer. Within the variety of styles evidenced in his many plays, however, stand key technical and conceptual loci which support his work as a whole, no matter what the veneer of the drama.

Those center points—essentially naturalistic in nature—will be taken up later in this discussion. But the puzzle of Peter Shaffer extends beyond mere technique or subject matter. In a larger frame of reference, there is difficulty in isolating the theoretical audience for whom he writes. Shaffer embodies that rare species of writer whose career straddles the worlds both of popular and "serious" drama. Impressive success on commercial stages has brought him enormous worldwide recognition, ready financial backing, and eagerness of top theater artists to work with him. *The Battle of Shrivings* (1970) alone of his dozen plays has failed to win an audience. *Yonadab* (1985), only a modest success, nonetheless ran for a year in repertory at the British National Theatre. All the rest of his works have received strong acclaim whenever they are performed. By most standards, Shaffer enjoys exceptional popularity on world stages and has earned his stature as one of our foremost writers.

Yet by no means does Shaffer pander to mass tastes to gain general audience following. Quite the contrary; his works involve intellectually demanding themes and innovative theatrical staging. Typically, at the center of his plays stands a questioning—or questing—protagonist, obsessed with discerning mankind's true metaphysical status. Shaffer's best known dramas—*The Royal Hunt of the Sun, Equus, Amadeus,* and *Yonadab*—feature heroes such as Pizarro, Dysart, Salieri, and Yonadab who probe their respective universes for answers to philosophical and theological puzzles. Eventually, each protagonist moves toward knowledge of God. At the same time, the hero seeks to discover how far man might assume the powers of God and *become* God—if indeed He exists. More than a hint of Promethian and Faustian hungers exist in his protagonists. Shaffer's underlying thrust in his major dramas resembles that found in ancient classical drama: to define the relationship of mortal man to immortal deity. Simultaneously, Shaffer's dramatic universe infers values mirroring today's God-is-dead intellectual system, thereby allying Shaffer with the existential world view as well. Small wonder that academics find it dicey to pigeonhole Shaffer as a proponent of a single vision. In his wide-ranging and eclectic thinking, he has few peers today, most of whom focus on psychological or social problems.

Nothing in Shaffer's family background mandated a career in the arts. Born in Liverpool on 15 May 1926, Peter Levin Shaffer and his identical twin brother Anthony grew up in a middle-class Jewish household. Jack Shaffer, a property company director, moved his wife Reka and the family to London in 1936. But with the start of the second world war, they moved frequently to evade the German bombers. Despite the ongoing war, Peter and Anthony attended prestigious St. Paul's School beginning in 1942. Both twins were accepted by Trinity College at Cambridge University; but satisfying their service obligations came first. In their case, they served as Bevin Boys, youths who dug coal in the mines of Kent.[1] In 1947 both Shaffers enrolled in Trinity College where they jointly edited the college paper.

Peter Shaffer came down from Cambridge in 1950 with a specialty in history but no definite career plans. Initially he tried his hand at various jobs until 1951 when he traveled to New York City. There, he worked for a book dealer, retail stores, and the New York Public Library. Shaffer later remarked that this period of his life was bleak and frustrating. But one positive outcome was his frequenting New York theaters. As a result of seeing so much theater, he felt encouraged to try writing plays, his first being "The Salt Land." Work in the business world provided him little satisfaction, and he returned to London in 1954 to work at a large music publishing house. While holding that position, Shaffer found his initial success in the realm of drama, when "The Salt Land" was telecast over ITV. Paradoxically, during this same period he also was establishing a reputation as a writer of fiction. He published three mystery novels in London and in the United States: *The Woman in the Wardrobe* (1951), *How Doth the Little Crocodile?* (1952), and *Withered Murder* (1955)—the latter two co-authored with his brother Anthony (the Tony-winning writer of *Sleuth*). In 1957, Shaffer had two more broadcast dramas aired—the unpublished radio play "The Prodigal Father" over BBC Radio and "Balance of Terror" (also unpublished) over BBC Television. Once his plays caught on, Shaffer never looked backward. Thereafter, he devoted his entire energies to the theater.

Shaffer's earliest full-length dramas, *Five Finger Exercise* (1958) and *The Royal Hunt of the Sun* (1964), immediately drew applause from critics who recognized a strong new voice in the theater. Awards came swiftly, initially in England and later in the United States, to confirm the importance of his writing to the modern stage. Later, *Equus* (1973) and *Amadeus* (1979) thoroughly won over audiences, earning both critical and popular applause. Both pieces became smash hits on Broadway, and each won a Tony Award as best drama. More recently, *Lettice & Lovage* (1987) received four Tony nominations, including one for best play. (Eventually the comedy won Tonys for Maggie Smith and Margaret Tyzack.) Thus, to this point Shaffer has established an enviable record of successes both commercially and critically.

Nor are Shaffer's plays solely popular on live stages. Movies have been made of nearly all his works to date. Here, the results are very mixed, however. Shaffer far prefers the stage medium to the screen, and readily admits the films of his works to be uneven. Interestingly, the factors that led to success or failure in transferring his plays to the screen—particularly the theatricality of his unique realism—also shed light on the nature of Shaffer's works themselves. Such a topic deserves separate consideration, and only a few points will be touched on here. But one unavoidable conclusion is that his plays, which are "exuberantly and unashamedly theatrical," have proven difficult to reconceive for the large screen.[2] Not surprisingly, the film director's task is easier with those works built on more conventional realism. One example may suffice. An interesting yet ultimately disappointing film of *Five Finger Exercise* was made in 1962. Despite an impressive cast (including Rosalind Russell, Maximilian Schell, and Jack Hawkins) the movie version never attains the psychological richness of the original stage production. However, because of the play's original naturalistic premises, the characterizations of the five principals, along with their fully delineated motivations, translate readily to a movie format.

Just how well *Five Finger Exercise* made the transformation to film—relatively speaking—becomes evident when considering Shaffer's dramas that move beyond realism in their original conception. A disastrous film adaptation of *Royal Hunt* (starring Christopher Plummer and Robert Shaw) followed in 1969, for instance. After viewing the hugely distorted movie made of his noble quest drama, Shaffer knew he no longer could entrust his plays to screen writers. Thereafter, he wrote the film scripts himself for *The Public Eye* (1972), *Equus* (1977), and *Amadeus* (1984). Considering how theater-oriented his pieces are in format and spirit, it is surprising that the movie versions fared as well as they did. There is proof that outstanding results are possible when the play transferences are achieved with imagination and flexibility. An example is Milos Forman's film of *Amadeus* which accumulated eight Academy Awards including Best Film of 1984 and Best Film Adaptation for Shaffer's movie script. Previously, Shaffer received an Oscar nomination for his film script of *Equus*—a movie whose graphic simulations during the horse-blinding scenes fatally compromised it at the box office.[3] As with *Royal Hunt*, the stage script for *Equus* prohibits its being reshaped for film in a literal fashion—a fact the director of the movie, Sidney Lumet, learned at a high price, according to Shaffer. On the more recent front, plans for a movie version of *Lettice & Lovage* are in the works, suggesting that the playwright remains open-minded about filmic versions of his works despite disappointments in the past. Additionally, unlike earlier statements denigrating movies, in a recent interview (see "A Conversation with Peter Shaffer [1990]" in this volume) Shaffer hinted that he might revise *Whom Do I Have the Honour of Addressing?* as a film. He even acknowledges that his most recent radio piece might also be an ideal candidate for a television play. The entire screen issue then remains open where Shaffer is concerned.

But to return to Shaffer's stage dramas, we need to delineate more closely the appeal of his ideas and techniques. Unlike the opaque conundrums underlying plays by certain other twentieth-century theater experimenters (Beckett and Pinter come to mind), Shaffer's dramas have remained accessible to the theater-going public. This fact tends to devalue his plays for politically oriented theorists who esteem a work according to its bewildering effect on audiences. For such detractors, to be "popular" with playgoers becomes an indictment of a play's worthiness. Only the puzzling, uncommercial, radical avant-garde retains merit for zealots like Brustein and Simon, accounting for their long and active distaste for Shaffer.[4]

Just as his success bridging artistic and popular values elicits mixed reactions, Shaffer evokes ambiguous response and controversy on dramaturgical grounds. If pressed to describe Shaffer's primary writing tools, however, most critics acknowledge the centrality of psychological naturalism. Conventional realism characterizes much of Shaffer's early work, including *Five Finger Exercise*, the one-act comedies, and the ill-fated *Battle of Shrivings* (1970, later rewritten as *Shrivings*, 1974). Although Shaffer temporarily returned to realism with *Lettice & Lovage* (1987) and the radio play *Whom Do I Have the Honour of Addressing?* (1989), naturalism never has been the playwright's favored dramatic approach. The initial draft for *The Royal Hunt of the Sun* already existed when the naturalistic *Five Finger Exercise* launched his career in 1958. His true inclinations lay in "big, sweeping theatre," as he explained to the interviewer D. Zerdin on BBC's "Profile" (11 September 1979). Shaffer elaborates in his Introduction to *The Collected Plays of Peter Shaffer* (New York: Harmony Books, 1982) that the times were not right for the unusual mannerisms of *Royal Hunt*. The tidal wave of realism during the

1950's, he declares, dictated that his early works follow standard conventions: "I became a playwright finally to be part of the grandiloquent and showy world of imaginative reality. It took me some time to acknowledge this to myself. The times, after all, scarcely favored such an ambition. The mid-1950s did not constitute a time when one could admit, with much chance of being sympathetically heard, a purpose to write about gods and grand aspirations, orators and ecstatics. It was a surging time for England, but the cry tended to be for social realism" (x).

Shaffer recognizes the value of representationalism, however. With this first success, he established his ability to write masterfully in the realistic mode. Shaffer states, "On balance, I feel I did crafted work in my first piece. It said what I wanted it to say, and it possessed a shape which made it play easily and finally accumulated its power" (viii). Shaffer's next plays—*Shrivings* and the one-act comedies *The Private Ear*, *The Public Eye*, *White Lies*, and *Black Comedy*—retained a realistic bias, thereby consolidating popularity with theater audiences. But careful observers of the stage understand that realism alone does not win audience support. His endeavors with realism permitted Shaffer to hone his talent for penetrating dialogue. The occasional intrusion of turgid prose and excessive sentimentality in *Five Finger Exercise* and in *Royal Hunt* largely was refined away in the crucible of this early period. Shaffer thus worked at and mastered dramatic realism with these works. Yet, good as these pieces played on stage, they did not satisfy what Peter Shaffer ultimately intended to achieve. *Five Finger Exercise* proved a valuable base from which he later could launch into more innovative theatrical enterprises.

Most crucial to Shaffer's dramatic style are the imaginative risks exhibited in his masterpieces. *The Royal Hunt of the Sun* (1964), *Equus* (1973), *Amadeus* (1979), and even the revised *Yonadab* (1985) all exhibit the daring theatrical techniques that make up the playwright's imprimatur. What makes the techniques fresh is his brilliant fusion of presentational narrative modes with traditional realism. The four dramas noted convey their respective stories through a system of narrative frameworks. At the outermost perimeter stand the plays' chorus-like narrators serving as moderators or masters of ceremony. Old Martin, Doctor Dysart, Salieri, and Yonadab address the audience from their posts, first as outside observers of the respective story lines; later, they will blend into the inner plot line as active participants. Though not entirely objective, each moderator as watcher enjoys a unique perspective that instantly engages the attention, interest, and curiosity of playgoers, drawing them into the action.[5] Illustrations from the plays will help. Old Martin, Pizarro's young aide in *Royal Hunt*, quickly gains audience interest when addressing them directly with his opening lines to the play:

> Save you all. My name is Martin. I'm a soldier of Spain and that's it. Most of my life I've spent fighting for land, treasure, and the cross. I'm worth millions. Soon I'll be dead, and they'll bury me out here in Peru, the land I helped ruin as a boy. This story is about ruin. Ruin and gold. . . . I'm going to tell you how one hundred and sixty-seven men conquered an empire of twenty-four million. (From *Collected Plays of Peter Shaffer*, p. 247—all quotations of Shaffer's plays come from this edition unless noted otherwise.)

Following his tantalizing come-on, Martin conjures flashback scenes through which Pizarro and other characters are introduced.

Parallel opening scenes mark all of Shaffer's finest dramas, whereby a narrator entices the audience into the world of the play. Dr. Dysart in the opening lines from *Equus* speaks directly to the audience while gesturing behind him at a youth, Alan Strang, nuzzling a horse standing next to him. The puzzling tableau is further heightened by the psychiatrist's cryptic words:

> With one particular horse, called Nugget, he embraces. The animal digs its sweaty brow into his cheek, and they stand in the dark for an hour—like a necking couple. And of all the nonsensical things—I keep thinking about the *horse!* (401)

*Amadeus* opens similarly with a non-realistic invocation. Following an "overture" comprised of stichomythic exposition whispered by two chorus figures, Salieri turns directly to the audience. He then entices his playgoers with an irresistible summons:

> *Vi Saluto! Ombri del Futuro! Antonio Salieri—a vostro*
> *servizio!*. . . . I can almost see you in your ranks—
> waiting for your turn to live. Ghosts of the Future! Be
> visible. I beg you. Be visible. Come to this dusty old
> room—this time, the smallest hours of dark November,
> eighteen hundred and twenty-three—and be my
> Confessors! (486–487)

Shaffer seems satisfied with the general template laid out here, for he turns again to its use in his most recent serious work, *Yonadab* (1985, heavily revised in 1987). Once he greets the audience at the start of *Yonadab*, the title protagonist begins to spin his web of enticing intrigue:

> This is a singularly unpleasant story. The Rabbis of the
> Middle Ages omitted it entirely, when they read out the
> scriptures, to spare the ears of their congregations—and
> they didn't know the half of it. I alone know it all—and,
> let me assure you, I don't intend to spare yours.[6]

In the four major plays, once having introduced himself and the general subject of the play, the narrator moves into the play circuitry where he assumes an active role in the enacted scenes of the story. At irregular intervals, the narrator breaks the illusion to comment often to the spectators about the scenic actions.[7] Such "breaks" in the story line allow for clarifying commentary on the plot, just as the omniscient observer in fiction uses stop-action to offer all-knowing remarks on the proceedings. But beyond that useful advantage, the narrator's "interruption" of the tale privileges him to fast-forward to later episodes in the story at will. The narrators—Martin, Dysart, Salieri, and Yonadab—become our guides as we traverse the actions of the plot, moving us faster or slower, directing our attention from one character to another, or from one detail to a second one.

Shaffer did not originate the narrator figure, of course. Witness Shakespeare's Richard the Second and Iago who also plot strategy for the audience before joining in the action. Similarly, tragic heroes in classical Greek drama often speak directly to the spectators. No one, however, develops the narrator character more effectively than Shaffer both as a story-telling device *and* as a fascinating figure unto himself. Use of the narrating "stage manager" also represents a hybrid version of presentational theater. For although the direct address to the audience cannot be considered realistic, the internal scenes introduced by the narrator are staged in what essentially is realism: characters communicate with each other through realistic dialogue, they move about the stage in conventional blocking, and the theatrical illusion is sustained for the duration of the scene being enacted. Shaffer thereby wrings important concessions from the realm of theatrical realism to gain flexibility in the narrative process.

Other non-representational modes emerge in the dramas of Peter Shaffer. Each of his four major works features striking iconographic sets and props to reinforce the substance of his themes. In *Royal Hunt*, the most stunning moments are evoked visually and through sound effects. Shaffer's stage directions to open scene 3 of the first act introduce the audience to the main visual emblem of the play:

> *The stage darkens and the huge medallion high on the back wall begins to glow. Great cries of "Inca!" are heard. Slowly the medallion opens outward to form a huge golden sun with twelve great inlaid rays. . . . In the center stands* ATAHUALLPA. (255)

Late in the play, that symbol of the sun is burned into the audience's memory during a scene called the Rape of the Sun; there, the greedy Spanish Conquistadors ravage the Incan emblem of gold to obtain its precious treasure. Again, the stage directions describe the non-verbal choreography involved:

> *Above, in the chamber, the treasure is piled up as before.* DIEGO *and the* CHAVEZ *brothers are seen supervising. They begin to explore the sun itself, leaning out of the chamber and prodding at the petals with their halberds. Suddenly* DIEGO *gives a cry of triumph, drives his halberd into a slot in one of the rays, and pulls out the gold inlay. The sun gives a deep groan, like the sound of a great animal being wounded. With greedy yelps, all the soldiers below rush at the sun and start pulling it to bits; they tear out the gold inlays and fling them on the*

> *ground, while terrible groans fill the air. In a moment*
> *only the great gold frame remains; a broken, blackened*
> *sun.* (291)

Other important moments in *Royal Hunt* form indelible imprints by
innovatively combining sound with panoramic image. In The Mime of
the Great Ascent (scene 8 of Act One), Shaffer conveys the sense of the
Spaniards climbing the high, frigid Andes mountains on their way to
meet Atahuallpa. Realistic depiction is abandoned for evocative
symbols and strange sounds:

> *As* OLD MARTIN *describes their ordeal, the men climb the*
> *Andes. It is a terrible progress: a stumbling, torturous*
> *climb into the clouds, over the ledges and giant chasms,*
> *performed to an eerie, cold music made from the thin*
> *whine of huge metal saws.* (266)

Soon, the bloody conjunction of the European and Incan worlds is
commemorated in The Mime of the Great Massacre that closes Act
One. With no spoken dialogue, Shaffer portrays the horror of the
Spaniards' betrayal of the Indians:

> *To a savage music, wave after wave of Indians are*
> *slaughtered and rise again to protect their lord, who*
> *stands bewildered in their midst. It is all in vain.*
> *Relentlessly the Spanish soldiers hew their way through*
> *the ranks of feathered attendants toward their quarry.*
> *They surround him . . . All the Indians cry out in horror.*
> *. . . [D]ragged from the middle of the sun by howling*
> *Indians, a vast bloodstained cloth bellies out over the*
> *stage. All rush off; their screams fill the theater. The*
> *lights fade out slowly on the rippling cloth of blood.*
> (277)

These illustrative passages only suggest the power of Shaffer's
presentational techniques. *The Royal Hunt of the Sun* most fully
embodies Shaffer's use of Epic and Total Theaters—modes advanced by
Bertolt Brecht and Antonin Artaud.[8]

Analogous scenes of powerful non-verbal theater exist in the remaining serious dramas. Like its predecessor, *Royal Hunt*, *Equus* constructs its fable with a fusion of highly articulate dialogue in the mode of naturalism, embedded in mind-stretching visual scenes drawing on expressionism. Indeed, the central set utilized in the drama speaks metaphorically to the audience at all times. Shaffer's description of the set starts by calling it "A square of wood set on a circle of wood" ("The Setting," *Equus*, in *The Collected Plays*, p. 399). By requiring that the backdrop for the set consist of tiers of seats on risers with both audience members and cast seated there, Shaffer intends that those persons serve functions in the play as "Witnesses, assistants—and especially a Chorus" (399). Shaffer's set instructions further suggest the square set resembles "A railed boxing ring" and a "dissecting theater" in an operating room. Such images are entirely appropriate for a plot that entails savage battle between the powers of orderly society and the chaotic impulse of instinctual religious worship.[9]

Horses, of course, play a key part in *Equus*, and Shaffer's choice of how to represent them on stage fairly well determines his overall theatrical approach. Shaffer is explicit in his stage directions that the horses only be portrayed abstractly. His descriptions of how actors are to play horses prohibit even the least element of realism. Brown-colored velvet tracksuits are to be worn by the actors, with matching gloves. On their feet are will be four-inch light-weight metal-braced lifts fastened to actual horseshoes. On their heads are large symbolic horse masks constructed of alternating strips of silver wire and leather, with no effort to hide the human head beneath.

Most telling of Shaffer's instructions about the horses is his mandate that "Any literalism which could suggest the cozy familiarity of a domestic animal—or worse, a pantomime horse—should be avoided. . . . Animal effect must be created entirely mimetically. . . . so that the masking has an exact and ceremonial effect" (400). The ritual base underlying *Equus* requires Alan Strang's orgiastic sessions of worship to be presentationally given. Only symbolic creatures and abstracted movements befit the play's theme. The result theatrically, however, is stunning. At the conclusion of the play's first act, Alan is hypnotized into reenacting his regular worship-rides on the horse Nugget. In Dysart's office, before the mesmerized psychiatrist, the boy activates the half dozen horse figures for his dream ride by calling out, "Equus—son of Fleckwus—son of Neckwus—*Walk*" (447). The rites which follow are described through stage directions:

> "*[A hum from the CHORUS. Very slowly the horses standing on the circle begin to turn the square by gently pushing the wooded rail. ALAN and his mount start to revolve. The effect, immediately, is of a statue being slowly turned round on a plinth. During the ride, however, the speed increases, and the light decreases until it is only a fierce spotlight on horse and rider, with the overspill glinting on the other masks leaning in toward them."]* (447).

All the while, Alan first croons, then shouts, instructions to the horse, projecting the lad's combined religious and sexual ecstacy that culminates in obvious spiritual and physical orgasm.

*Equus* contains an equally spectacular finale which relies on symbolic actions using presentationalism. Alan's attempt to make love with Jill at the stables is interrupted by what the boy believes to be Equus' warning from the adjacent stall. His sexual desire totally squelched by religious guilt, Alan brutally dismisses the girl and prepares to answer Equus' demands for obeisance. During this abreacted scene inspired by Dysart's promises for his total recovery, Alan exhibits through his actions why he stabbed out the eyes of six horses: Alan's hopes for a normal sexual life was blocked by his self-designed religion making Equus his personal god. The lad knows of no other choice:

> ALAN [*in terror*]:  Eyes! . . . White eyes—never closed!
> Eyes like flames—coming—coming!
> . . . God seest! God seest! . . . NO!
> . . . . No more. No more, Equus
> . . . .Equus . . . Noble Equus. . .
> Faithful and True. . . God-slave . . .
> Thou—God—Seest—NOTHING!
>
> [*He stabs out NUGGET's eyes. The horse stamps in agony. A great screaming begins to fill the theater, growing ever louder. ALAN dashes at the other two horses and*

> *blinds them too, stabbing over the rails. . . . The*
> *screams increase. The other horses follow into the*
> *square. The whole place is filled with cannoning, blinded*
> *horses. . . .*] (474)

As in *Royal Hunt,* Shaffer turns to traditional realism, with its highly explicit and articulate dialogue, to promote plot and characterization for much of *Equus.* But for the climactic moments in the plot, the playwright provides emblematic scenes in which visual and aural effects move audience intellects—and emotions—beyond what is possible through stage literalism. Those remarkable stage images epitomize the glory of Shaffer's playwriting.

Of all that Shaffer has written to date, *Amadeus* elicits the most praise for its dramaturgical strengths. As in *Royal Hunt* and *Equus,* Shaffer punctuates his major scenes in *Amadeus* with haunting theatrical effects to create an unforgettable picture. And as in all his dramas, he consciously designs symbolic moments to conclude each act. Moreover, the epiphanous scenes represent far more than riveting moments appealing to the audience's visual and aural senses. Shaffer in those episodes succeeds brilliantly in embodying crucial truths in a single image. He does so by the imaginative melding of realistic speech with abstract image. The result is the coalescence of previous story understanding into a new, revelatory whole.

The most dazzling scene of enlightenment in *Amadeus* occurs at the close of Act One. By this point in the story, Antonio Salieri, principal musician in Emperor Joseph II's court in Vienna, has come to fear the musical genius of his younger rival Mozart. To measure the threat represented by the upstart newcomer, Salieri coerces Mozart's wife into bringing him Mozart's manuscripts of works-in-progress. Once Salieri begins to read the written musical scores, the sounds of actual music are heard in the theater to designate what he was reading. Shaffer not only has solved the logistics of allowing his audience to share the music Salieri hears in his head; the dramatist also mounts an electric experience on stage to suggest how transcendent the moment stands in musical history.

An analysis of this single scene reflects Shaffer's innovative mind at work. He first needs to have Salieri become aware of the immensity of Mozart's genius. Once that amazing fact has sunk in,

Salieri must be made to revolt against God's ordained design. Using a two-part schema, the dramatist first stuns Salieri with Mozart's music itself. The stage directions interweave with Salieri's monologue to forge the climactic moment in his life:

> [. . . *He contemplates the music lying there as if it were a*
> *great confection he is dying to eat, but dare not. Then*
> *suddenly he snatches at it—tears the ribbon—opens the*
> *case and stares greedily at the manuscripts within.*
> *Music sounds instantly, faintly, in the theater, as his eye*
> *falls on the first page. It is the opening of the* Twenty-
> Ninth Symphony, *in A Major. Over the music, reading*
> *it.]*
>
> SALIERI:  She had said that these were his original scores.
>                    First and only drafts of the music. Yet they
>                    looked like fair copies. They showed no
>                    corrections of any kind. . . . Displace one note
>                    and there would be diminishment. Displace one
>                    phrase and the structure would fall. *[He resumes*
>                    *reading, and the music also resumes: a*
>                    *ravishing phrase from the slow movement of*
>                    *the* Concerto for Flute and Harp.*]* . . . The truth
>                    was clear. That serenade had been no accident.
>                    . . . I was staring through the cage of those
>                    meticulous ink strokes at an Absolute Beauty!
>                    (518–519)

To represent how devastating this new understanding is to Salieri, Shaffer instructs the composer to fall into a swoon. The question then arises, what will—or can—Salieri do about the situation with Mozart? With that unspoken query in the audience's collective mind, Shaffer shifts into the scene's second part: Salieri's new resolve. Upon regaining consciousness, lying amidst the fallen manuscripts of Mozart's compositions, Salieri *"addresses his God"*:

> *Capisco!* I know my fate. Now for the first time I feel my
> emptiness as Adam felt his nakedness . . . *Grazie,*
> *Signore!* You gave me the desire to serve you—which
> most men do not have—then saw to it the service was
> shameful in the ears of the server. . . . *Why? . . . What is*

> *my fault?* . . . . I have worked and worked the talent you
> allowed me. . . . Solely that in the end, in the practice of
> the art which alone makes the world comprehensible to
> me, I might hear Your Voice! And now I do hear it—and it
> says only one name: MOZART! . . . . Spiteful,
> sniggering, conceited, infantine Mozart! . . . .
> *[Savagely.] Grazie e grazie ancora! [Pause]* So be it! From
> this time we are enemies, You and I! I'll not accept it
> from You. (519–520)

And with Salieri's audacious challenge to God, Shaffer closes the first half of his drama. The overall design now is apparent, and the remainder of the play will chronicle Salieri's failed attempt to defeat his deity.

Nothing from the second act achieves quite the equivalent excitement, although the bizarre death scene of Mozart is highly charged as he discovers Salieri's machinations. Salieri's attempted suicide near the end also provides striking visual pictures that reenforce the final frustrated acts of the deranged court composer. Ironically, the emblematic scene which best counterbalances the close of Act One does not appear in Shaffer's play text but rather in his movie script for *Amadeus*. There, a new, important episode is added to depict Mozart— on his deathbed—dictating to Salieri the unfinished score to his *Requiem Mass*. Though the added movie scene attains enormous dramatic power, the actions it proposes are wholly fictitious and incredible. In the stage script proper, the final graphic moment showing Salieri proves powerful enough: he stands before us—an aged, crazed, but still shrewd conniver—arms outspread to welcome us into his brotherhood of Mediocrities.

Shaffer's next drama was *Yonadab* (1985), his fable of human evil and aspirations drawn from Biblical accounts. Given the dark and foreboding tenor of the play, the initial emblematic scene seems entirely suitable. Again, the episode appears near the end of the opening act. Here, another complete scene (scene 8) follows before the act actually concludes. But for all practical purposes, little additional exposition or plot development can occur after the hair-raising events of scene 7.

The plot, in brief, concerns the devilry of King David's errant nephew Yonadab in Jerusalem long before the Christian era. Beginning with facts from Samuel 2 in the Old Testament, Shaffer fashions another god-seeking protagonist.[10] In the case of Yonadab, though he aspires to godhead, he hungers first for finite proof of God's existence. One of his tactics to "flush out God" is to challenge Him on every front. Yonadab gradually convinces his cousin Amnon, heir apparent to David's throne, that Amnon can take whatever he desires and thereby define his godhead. Yonadab, meanwhile, stands on the sideline to watch as those he dupes attempt to become earthly deities through arrogant actions usually reserved for gods alone.

When he confesses to Yonadab that he wants more than anything to sexually possess his half-sister Tamar, Amnon is actively encouraged by Yonadab. Tamar is tricked into going to Amnon's palace and even to his bedroom, under the ruse of his being very ill. Once alone with her, Amnon reveals his true intentions to have her. She remains obdurate to his seduction, and Amnon quickly loses patience and rapes her. Yonadab is the voyeur *par excellence*, and he locates himself near the bed chamber to observe. Unexpectedly, Amnon drops the curtains surrounding the bed, leaving Yonadab the mere watcher of blurred shadows on the curtains. Shaffer ingeniously constructs a visual version of a momentous event in ancient history—all through a narrated account of shifting shadows. Yonadab is the audience's guide to a deed that ultimately leads to the demise of David's house and unrivalled empire:

> *(With increasing visibility the shadows of their bodies are thrown on to the curtain: immense black shapes enlarged and distorted by the lamps. During the following speech they make a series of abstract and strange shapes: a mysterious procession of glyphs.)*
> *(To audience)* All my life I remembered what I saw that night: the shadows!—more terrible than bodies. The limbs thrown up on the curtains like the letters of some grotesque language formed long, long before writing. There on the fall of a Jerusalem drape I saw, writ enormous . . . the archaic alphabet of the Book of Lust. (127, from *Lettice and Lovage* and *Yonadab* [London: Penguin Books, 1989]. All quotations from *Yonadab* will be taken from this edition)

In *Yonadab* as in the other dramas considered here, the unique achievement of Shaffer's writing involves the surprising merger of realistic and presentational elements that usually remain antithetical to one another. Thus, even as Yonadab narrates the dreadful results of his plottings with Amnon, Tamar, and Absalom, Shaffer knows to insert a visual cameo to underscore the situation emblematically:

> *(Low music sounds. From high above descends the corpse of* ABSALOM *hanging by its long black hair.)*
> YONADAB: *(To audience)* Absalom died later—caught in a tree by his famous hair, fleeing the wrath of his father.
> *(*KING DAVID *appears, his head under a prayer shawl. The* HELPERS *depart.)*
>> The father mourned his eldest son, of course—but the mourning for Absalom far exceeded the mourning for Amnon. It was the hardest pain of his life. . . . I saw all their transports, this royal family, their lusts for transcendence—and I saw nothing. Always the curtain was between us. (181)

Parallel to Shaffer's other dramas, the passage just noted appears at the conclusion of *Yonadab*, serving as a neat sum-up of the entire play, thanks to articulate, realistic narrative joined to an unforgettable visual emblem.

Finally, lest we think Shaffer's patented curtain closers occur only with his serious plays, consider for a moment his comedy *Lettice & Lovage* (1987). Several features are found in *Lettice & Lovage* that resemble those of the more serious drama; but for now we shall focus on the crucial curtain scenes, particularly those ending the first two acts.[11] Act One closes with the tour guide Lettice Douffet fired by her superior at the Preservation Trust, Lotte Schoen. Their "exit interview" had been free-wheeling, and the contrasting views of the two women openly aired. Although she had tried to explain her infelicities with facts concerning the provincial estate of which she was tour guide, Lettice realized in advance that her attempts would be futile. Therefore, when Lotte indeed dismissed her, Lettice was ready. With great august bearing, Lettice likens herself to Queen Mary just before her execution

by Elizabeth. Lettice asks her exeutioner Lotte if she recalled what
Queen Mary had worn on that auspicious day:

> LETTICE:    Queen Mary appeared in a dress of deepest
>             black. But when her ladies removed this from
>             her—what do you imagine was revealed?
> LOTTE:      I really can't guess.
>                             . . . .
> LETTICE:    . . . A full-length shift was seen. A garment
>             the color of the whoring of which she had
>             been accused! The color of martyrdom—and
>             defiance! *Blood red!*
>
> *[She steps out of her cloak to reveal a brilliant red ankle-
> length nightdress, embossed all over with little golden
> crowns . . .]*
>
>             Yes—all gasped with the shock of it! All
>             watched with unwilling admiration—that
>             good old word again—all watched with
>             *wonder* as that frail captive, crippled from
>             her long confinement, stepped out of the
>             darkness of her nineteen years' humiliation
>             and walked into eternity—a totally self-
>             justified woman! (32, from *Lettice & Lovage*
>             [New York: Harper & Row, 1990].
>             Quotations are taken from this edition.)

The graphic gesture of a doomed woman, metaphorically thumbing her
nose at her captors, precisely matches Lettice's circumstances.

Lettice's black cloak figures in the emblem scene closing the
play's second act, as well. By now in the plot, Lettice and Lotte are
becoming good friends—with the help of "quaff," a strong brew Lettice
alleges to be of Renaissance origin. Lotte even reveals that she wears a
wig, showing how much a confidante Lettice has become. The women
decide to eat out, and Lettice urges her colleague to leave her wig off
when they leave to dine. After a hesitation, Lotte agrees:

> LOTTE:    Very well . . . I will.
> *[They look at each other. Then LETTICE laughs, a clear
> bright laugh of perception, and walks away across the
> room. She laughs again.]*

> What is it? What are you thinking?
> *[But instead of replying,* LETTICE *takes off her black cloak and lays it ceremoniously at the base of the staircase, in the manner of Sir Walter Raleigh assisting Queen Elizabeth.]*
> LETTICE:    Come, madame. Your hedgehogs await! (61)

Again, a picture is worth the proverbial thousand words. In both emblem scenes, the logical and literal factors of the moment are fused with an apt pictorial rendition to effect striking theatrical results.

Nowhere among his plays does Peter Shaffer venture far from his personal version of "realism." That fact perhaps should not surprise playgoers, because Shaffer's dialogue stands with the finest written in our times. And articulate language, after all, is "literal" in all senses of that term. But Shaffer is not content with a single dramaturgical strength; his imagination reaches outward to encompass visual displays of literal thought. Nor are the graphic equivalents to realistic details limited to mere symbols on stage. Shaffer, with the help of equally innovative directors such as John Dexter and Peter Hall, stretches to embody spectacular but always intelligent theatrical techniques, as we have seen.

If we seek to isolate one specific attribute that defines Peter Shaffer's genius, then, we could do worse than to choose the methods chronicled here: the masterful merging of the literalism of realism with the provocative of the abstract pictorial. Shaffer's power derives from a type of "trans-literalism" that invites the shorthand of stage emblems. No other playwright today can claim such an achievement.

# Notes

1. Full details concerning Shaffer's youth may be found in Gene A. Plunka, *Peter Shaffer: Roles, Rites, and Rituals in the Theater* (Rutherford, N.J.: Fairleigh Dickinson Univ. Press, 1988). Also, see my forthcoming book *Peter Shaffer* from Macmillan (UK) in 1991.

2. Clare Colvin, "Quest for Perfection," *Drama*, No. 159 (1986): 12.

3. Useful comment on this entire issue is found in C. J. Gianakaris, "Drama into Film: The Shaffer Situation," *Modern Drama*, 28, No. 1 (1985): 83–98.

4. See, for example, Mervyn Rothstein, "Passionate Beliefs Renew a Fight over Art and Profit," *New York Times*, 15 May 1990, Sec. B, pp. 1–2.

5. Comparable narrator-protagonists occasionally have appeared on world stages, as in Brecht's *The Good Woman of Setzuan* and Robert Bolt's *A Man for All Seasons*; Shakespeare perhaps employed such a joint character most fully with the figure of Richard the Third.

6. From *Lettice and Lovage* and *Yonadab* (London: Penguin Books, 1989), p. 87.

7. Old Martin represents a slightly different case. Martin, as older man, appears at the play's beginning, at its end, and occasionally throughout. But because he tells of events in Peru when he was a boy, Martin in the story line proper is played by a youthful version of himself— another, younger actor altogether called Young Martin. In a shorter play, the presence of two Martins on stage would not be a drawback because spectators would encounter no problem in keeping the two characters straight; however, in *Royal Hunt* the large cast sometimes confuses audiences regarding the two Martin parts. In *Equus* there is no problem because the actions Dysart narrates seemingly occurred in the near past, a circumstance duplicated by Yonadab and his tale, as well. Shaffer solved the time shifts effectively for *Amadeus*. There, Salieri smoothly alters his appearance by disguises, from agedness to youth and back again, while continuing to address the audience.

8. An informative and full discussion of the influence of Brecht and Antonin Artaud on Shaffer's plays is available in Gene A. Plunka's book cited above.

9. I have discussed the ramifications of the set for *Equus* elsewhere in "Theatre of the Mind in Miller, Osborne and Shaffer," *Renascence*, 30, No. 1 (1977): 33–42.

10. Shaffer freely acknowledges, however, an equally essential influence in his writing of *Yonadab*. The playwright had read with great interest the 1970 novel *The Rape of Tamar* by the South African writer Dan Jacobson (New York: Macmillan). Jacobson's book contains many of the

features Shaffer was to use, including making Yonadab's the central perspective for the narration.

11. The emblem scene closing the original version of *Lettice and Lovage* also matched the summary qualities of which we have spoken. But to make the overall story line more logical, Shaffer changed the ending and so dropped the marvelous visual effect of a petard being readied for battle against London's philistine establishment. Incidentally, the deleting in *Lettice and Lovage* of the conjunction "and" and its replacement with an ampersand (as in *Lettice & Lovage*) occurred when the revised play opened on Broadway in March of 1990.

# A CONVERSATION WITH
# PETER SHAFFER (1990)

On 23 March 1990—during the final previews of *Lettice & Lovage* at the Ethel Barrymore Theatre in New York prior to its 25 March Broadway opening—C. J. Gianakaris spent several hours in conversation with Peter Shaffer in the playwright's Manhattan apartment home. The remarks that follow are the result. Gianakaris, who also was present at the comedy's London premiere late in 1987, begins the discussion with questions about the revised version of *Lettice & Lovage* which assumed the ampersand in the title for the American production. Soon after these conversations, *Lettice & Lovage*, its author, the director, and the two lead actresses all were nominated for Tony Awards. Maggie Smith and Margaret Tyzack went on to win Tonys for best leading actress and best supporting actress, respectively. (Editor's Note)

GIANAKARIS: Let us start with the very unfortunate delay of the opening here of *Lettice & Lovage* which initially was scheduled to open on Broadway early in 1989. It would seem to be—to have been—quite dispiriting for all of you.

SHAFFER: Maggie Smith, you know, late in 1988 was the victim of an accident in which she fell from a bicycle and shattered her shoulder very badly. The doctor called it a monstrous fracture. She also suffers from Graves' Disease, an illness of the thyroid which gave her a lot of trouble with her eyes; she's had two operations for that. We've had quite a delay. It is dispiriting in a way, yes, because things tended a little to cut off the boil, as you can imagine. But we're very much on the boil again. In one way there's been an advantage. I think that in some ways the *Lettice & Lovage* production is better here than in London. First, it has the benefit of the new ending which it might not

*25*

have used if we had not waited. (Yet we probably would have done the revised script anyway because we had used it in London when Geraldine McEwan took over for Maggie Smith). In any event, I think that it may have been harder for Maggie Smith to have gone directly from one ending to another after playing the first version for a solid year in England.

We also have the benefit of its looking better here. It's handsome in the house [the Barrymore Theatre]; it looks good and is beautifully lit. I've not altered it for American audiences and tastes except in the obvious ways. I've done very little. I've put in the new ending and a few new bits here and there. But on the whole it's much the same text that was seen in the London premiere of 1987. So, it wasn't *that* dispiriting, finally. One simply went about one's other work.

GIANAKARIS: Maggie Smith is quite a plucky person, it would seem.

SHAFFER: Yes, she's very courageous. I think that courage is a *sine qua non* of being a great actress; I think courage is one of the gifts given you at your christening, because one can be endowed with many other gifts—like talent—that may not come to fruition if you haven't got courage—sheer fortitude.

GIANAKARIS: And Margaret Tyzack was willing to hold tight during the forced delay?

SHAFFER: Yes, but it was dismaying for her too because she had, I imagine, pencilled in an extended period of work from the production—if we were lucky enough to run for a year or so here. Then, after the accident, she had suddenly, I suppose, to look for new work. It's never a pleasure for an actor to do that.

GIANAKARIS: Obviously, *Lettice & Lovage* depends on crucial dynamics between the two leads for its ultimate effectiveness. How much of those dynamics do you believe will be conveyed when other performers take the roles perhaps down the line?

SHAFFER: It is difficult to speak of performers whom one has not yet seen. I think it's very important, but I think the same is true of any performance of any play, particularly when you are dealing with two actors involved with scenes that depend on two equal performance levels—whether it's *Romeo and Juliet* or *Lettice & Lovage*—or whatever. Surely it's true of all performances everywhere. There was quite good rapport between Geraldine McEwan and Sara Kestleman in London after they replaced Maggie Smith and Margaret Tyzack. Sara was a very good Lotte, partly because of her continental background that suggested a European past. It worked very well there—the chemistry between her and Geraldine McEwan.

GIANAKARIS: Speaking about becoming dispirited, theater followers must be very disillusioned by now with respect to the fate of your 1985 drama *Yonadab*. Its initial reception at its London premiere was mixed, to be sure. But it enjoyed a good run at the National. Then, you thoroughly revised, almost rewrote, the play [now published by Penguin Books in England]. A New York opening had been announced for late 1988 with Sir Peter Hall again to direct as he had in England. I recall that casting difficulties delayed its going into production, and then problems with Peter Hall finding available time to direct the new production. Subsequently, nothing more has been heard about *Yonadab*. What seems to be the next step on that front?

SHAFFER: Production—if we can ever get one. Once it was clear Peter Hall no longer had time free, I had hoped Adrian Noble was going to direct, because he likes the play so much. Of course, then he was appointed new head of the Royal Shakespeare Company and obviously now can't do *Yonadab* because of his enormous work load in his new capacity. So we had to look elsewhere. It's a great shame, since the several delays now have led to the passing of valuable time.

GIANAKARIS: Yes, it is. In my view the revised version is exceptionally strong—very imaginative and possessed of potential for fine theatrical magic. In certain ways, the new script reminds one of the innovative use of non-individualized characters in various roles in *Equus*.

SHAFFER: I'd love to see it done. Patrick Stewart—who played King David in the original production and then went on to do the role of Yonadab after Alan Bates left the cast—wanted to do a staged reading in Los Angeles. But nothing seems to have come of that idea either.

GIANAKARIS: What would be the benefit of a staged reading of *Yonadab*?

SHAFFER: It would benefit me. You learn a great deal when the text is out of your hand and on the tongues of other people, actors. It's rather frustrating, this delay with *Yonadab*, but one must press on. I

would like to see it done. The theater even in England is not
particularly enterprising. If a thing hasn't "worked" in a central
situation like the National Theatre, you don't get requests from many
repertory companies or good provincial houses, and I can't think why.
They just want to do the clearcut successes. That appears to be very
unenterprising of them. I do fault the repertory houses in England.

Since *Shrivings* first appeared in print [Shaffer's radically revised
version of his 1970 drama *The Battle of Shrivings*], I think it's had one
performance at the New York Festival. They've given up, the whole
length and breadth of England. And yet they're always whining about
finding new material—yet they just want to do the clear successes.
They do *Equus* and they do *Amadeus*, but they don't do anything that
didn't work—in their view—in London. It's baffling to me, and I'm
very disillusioned about the situation, because it seems to me that they
are being cowardly, playing safe in an enormous way.

GIANAKARIS: A comparable charge has been directed at
Broadway, except that some plays which don't succeed there have been
picked up by outside rep theaters willing to take risks. In different
venues, those works are tried and sometimes do rather well.

SHAFFER: It is possible to do *Yonadab* in a regional situation
and then to bring it into New York. One could do it that way around.
But consider that we don't even have a director and so we can't get the
lead actor. I wasn't particularly successful in finding a Yonadab in the
auditioning process in the last few years. It is frustrating. We did finally
find someone who might have done it, but he was never given a chance
when the whole thing fell apart over Peter Hall's dates of availability to
direct.

GIANAKARIS: On another matter, so much of the dialogue
being written today is loaded with crypto-jargon. What do you think
future prospects to be for literate dialogue—such as your own?

SHAFFER: I don't know. In the limited future, I think people
will still celebrate what you call "literate dialogue." I notice in the
previews of *Lettice* that the pleasure of the audience seems to derive
from hearing finished sentences. But in the remote future, I am much
more pessimistic. It seems to me that what the English language needs
is for a vast army of people on both sides of the Atlantic who cared
about it. I don't mean that they should set themselves against fresh

usage. But we live in a culture that is quite literally cultivating illiteracy.

I'm not speaking about interesting slang. But at the supermarket you will find written on the package of your milk the words "skim milk," because a lot of people can't hear all the letters in the word "skimmed," especially those persons for whom English is not their first language. I was in the supermarket recently, and there was a sign over one of the aisles reading "chill drinks." There of course is an adjective "chill," but this sign meant "chilled." It's a small segment of a large, important circle. These are not instances of interesting slang. This just reflects persons who are indifferent to grammar. You can't blame them all. For some minorities who come to this country, language is simply a utilitarian tool used to make their living—to hold down jobs and to feed their families. But for anyone caring for language, it is dispiriting to see it being laid to waste like this.

In popular movies, of course, there's no language left. I once actually reduced language required for caper movies or for the Indiana Jones-type adventure movies—stuff turned out for American teenagers, to only two words: O-M-Y-G-A-A-W-D—"Oh, my god!" The other one could be spelled L-E-Z-G-I-T-O-W-D-A-H-E-E-R—"Let's get outa here!" If you possess a mastery of these two terms, that's all you will need to write a movie script—with various grunts in between.

GIANAKARIS: This is what I meant in terms of appropriate actors for *Yonadab*. It would take an exceptional actor to be able to bite into and extract and emit in understandable form the stretches of articulate dialogue in the script. We don't seem trained to be able to handle such language now.

SHAFFER: No, we're not anymore.

GIANAKARIS: I recall from previous talks together that you believe television has conditioned us to the twelve-minute scene unit before a commercial comes on. Our thought processes now don't seem capable of being stretched beyond those short limits at this time.

SHAFFER: The time span is ever decreasing, from eight then to four minutes. And now these sound bites of only seconds heard in political news broadcasting. It's unbelievable. British dramatist Simon Gray recently had a brilliant television play performed on the Arts & Entertainment Network. But the commercial breaks were so numerous that the plot became unfollowable. I wrote a letter to the A & E Network producers, because I found the intrusions outrageous, especially where Gray's gothic thriller was concerned. Of course, I got no reply. I wonder if a writer knows what happens to his work when it is sold over here—that it will be sliced up like salami and served to the American public in tiny, bite-sized chunks.

GIANAKARIS: Do you think that there are certain topics, issues, and themes which deserve special treatment by playwrights right now?

SHAFFER: Yes, some that are not treated at all—the taboos of our world. I think that nobody sufficiently addresses himself to the total disparagement by our civilization of its own achievements. I think it astounding that you can read statements in the press—such as those by the Board of Education in this city—that advocate stressing Afro-American studies and Oriental studies to the exclusion or downgrading (some professors say) of Western culture. I think that is what the French call a betrayal by the intelligentsia—by the people who should know better—of something they should be guarding and celebrating. There is a gigantic play or plays in all this. I don't mind being called a conservative if by that you mean I recognize what the human race has *most* and *best* achieved and then want to preserve it. To conserve something is not an altogether bad thing anyway.

I'm lucky enough to have inherited a culture of the utmost complexity. Take, say, the early 1800's: what was happening in the West—Goethe was writing his Faust, Beethoven was composing his quartets, Goya was painting the black paintings? During the same period, what was happening in Nigeria at this point? Whatever it was, should it be celebrated over Goethe, Beethoven, and Goya? There is a very passionate subject here to me—the way we are pissing on our own culture. We are seeking ways to commit suicide.

GIANAKARIS: Are politics perhaps dominating the arts and institutions today?

SHAFFER: I could see that deans of colleges have a very mixed student body. The act of assimilating—making a multi-racial society become one society—is perhaps possible. But it's not going to be done by saying we should teach black studies to the exclusion of white achievements or by false pretensions—to pretend as I often read that throughout the centuries African music, for example, is the equivalent or as good as the music of Mozart or Mendelssohn or Schumann and others. That's an untruth, a lie being told to the young. And I care more about that than anything else.

GIANAKARIS: You are presuming that criteria exist—something under attack these days.

SHAFFER: This is one theme that needs to be treated by drama, it seems to me. Talk about the "decline of the West," this is a *self-willed* decline of the West. I'm not a racist at all; I simply like truth. There is nothing unique in acknowledging accomplishments by persons of other races or cultures. We all live by things achieved by other cultures, at other times.

GIANAKARIS: I sense that there are more political polemics in English and European drama than perhaps in America. A hit play in Europe must have a sharp edge to it—must be urgently advancing some cause or radical concept. Peter Handke on the continent and David Hare in England come to mind.

SHAFFER: I don't understand Hare's plays. Individually, the scenes are good. But they don't finally add up to me. I couldn't understand *Secret Rapture*. Everyone said that it was an attack on Thatcherite England; I didn't see that it was at all. I just saw a caricature of a conservative lady. The play didn't reach me. I didn't understand why the girl was rejecting a fine, intelligent, affectionate, faithful, and attractive man in favor of a completely neurotic and tiresome woman. I didn't understand it at all; I just sat there bemused. I don't say that Hare was uninteresting, because he is a good dramatist. He "dramatizes" very well. But the play finally didn't "feed" me at all. I sat there empty and baffled as I have done before—as with *Plenty*.

GIANAKARIS: Who are some of the directors and authors on the continent who perhaps interest you at the moment?

SHAFFER: I wish I had more time to look into them. It seems a comparative easy thing to attack things that work—that you attack things others popularly attack, like Yuppies and junk bondists and people like that. And I think such figures should be attacked. But I don't really find the attacks particularly effective, much of the time. I'm not sure that *Easy Money* for instance was an especially trenchant attack on all that; it consisted mainly of several people shouting four-letter words. I admire *One Man Show* which I thought a better political play than many a tract-ish piece I've seen done. I've enjoyed *Pravda* when Anthony Hopkins played the lead, finding it like a great political cartoon.

GIANAKARIS: Do you think the European Community, once it all comes together, will greatly affect the arts and especially theater in any given way?

SHAFFER: Yes, I believe so. Everything should be revitalized by the communication of cultures; the mingling should be marvelous. It hasn't happened much yet, though. I find English drama remains doggedly English, and French drama, such as it is, doggedly French. Oddly enough, the Mediterranean countries don't appear to have much playwriting at all. That's partly because so much of their "drama" happens openly in the streets. Somehow, the north seems to produce more drama—the more introverted cultures. The Italians, Spaniards, and Greeks tend more to act out their lives in the open air and in their religions. Of course, all this may change.

GIANAKARIS: Will England truly become part of the European Community?

SHAFFER: I hope so. It has to be. It has no other destiny. It is no longer anything without the rest of Europe. England's reluctance to accept the inevitable is understandable because the English have had 1,000 years as an island, and as a very powerful, magnificent island.

GIANAKARIS: The British are protesting the "chunnel," the railroad line being constructed beneath the English Channel.

SHAFFER: Yes, but I can understand that, too. The tunnel is a violation of their sense of insularity, in the good sense as well as in the bad sense. There is something perversely fine about being an island from which, though very small, enormous things happened all over the world. The national fear is to be absorbed into a large commune with a unified currency and a blurring of the lines. I always have sympathized with the phrase *vive la difference* —it's very important to me. I love difference. I'm not at all happy with the idea of one world in the sense that everything is homogenized. In America, you can travel 200 miles to arrive in the town you just left, thanks in part to malls. The Americans are devoted to making the world "one" world—the one world the average American tourist can understand. Put out a bit of plastic and enjoy it. That is understandable, too. In fact, one thing will happen—must happen—now that England is a small and poorer country that has lost its hegemony and lost its destiny. To escape a desperately neurotic old age England must join in a new venture, to forget all its old mind sets, and get on with something else. It must use the extraordinary British talent for survival, ingenuity, and many, many imaginative virtues it possesses in a new way. Because the alternative is too bleak: a nation isolated from the centers of power which obviously are the United States, Japan, and nascent Germany, having very little contact with the rest of the world. Living off its past, it can only become increasingly neurotic. Countries go mad as well as people. That would be disastrous. We live in a tragic world, because a resounding right course like that is purchased by the surrender of things that are very valuable: the individuality of a country. The trick will be, if it can be worked, to preserve our individuality at the same time that we all join up together.

GIANAKARIS: There is a particular pattern one finds in your plays: not the total absence but a very limited expression of romantic love. One simply finds little love, and when it is found, it is represented in a very pragmatic form. In some cases, the love is cynical, as seen all the way back in *Five Finger Exercise*. The single scene of unbridled passion in *Yonadab* centers on a brutal rape. And nearly all instances of romantic passion lead to unhappy results. Is there in you a play that will use romance in another key?

SHAFFER: Yes, I would like to write such a romantic play. But it is very difficult to do. Look at the great body of dramatic work over the centuries: how many romantic plays do you know that succeed? *Romeo and Juliet*. Name another.

GIANAKARIS: *Antony and Cleopatra* is another.

SHAFFER: Yes, that's two. It's very interesting that the dramatist in both examples is forced to invent division to keep the lovers going. The balcony scene in *Romeo and Juliet* was invented entirely, because without it the story would be over by the second act. From the dramatist's perspective, had their love been consummated then, all the rest would run downhill. They are kept apart so that the play can go on. It's very inspired of Shakespeare to use that balance thusly. And of course Antony keeps leaving Cleopatra to go about the political business of the world, to go to Rome to marry Octavia, to go fight battles. Love is an estate we always want to be in; but paradoxically our watching two people honeying and making love dramatically loses power very quickly unless something conspires to interrupt it or stoke it up.

It has always puzzled me greatly that the two leading emotions in life are love and hate—and that the two great interests of the world are love and death. I know very few plays that deal with these themes, interestingly. *Macbeth* is a terrifying and brilliant play about the consequences of being a murderer. I'm not sure I know another such work in modern literature. I don't know a great play about murder. I know a lot of thrillers, but I don't know a great drama about someone falling in love.

In another sense, I truly meant my comedy *Lettice & Lovage* to be about love, because in fact—though obviously not in a sexual way—Lettice seduces everyone she meets: she seduces Lotte Schoen to her appreciation of life, and she seduces Bardolph from his wintery profession into something wholly different. That's not love in the romantic sense, but it is love of the spirit.

GIANAKARIS: Your plays deal with affection and bonding but on a more ecumenical basis that avoids reservations regarding gender. In those works, we all recognize a world of multiple relationships.

SHAFFER: There is a kind of mockery in Shakespeare of love. There also is an acknowledgment of its enviable situation. Shakespeare knew more about love than anybody, really. What are the sonnets if they aren't a deep, trenchant analysis of everything involved with falling in love, from being in love. And that includes all the attendant unease of disturbance and jealousy and defeats.

GIANAKARIS: Can you comment on the process of transferring your plays from London (where most first opened) to New York, or in the case of *White Lies* from New York to London?

SHAFFER: I don't find much difficulty with those transferences at all. Those who speak of problems in opening dramas in different venues usually are talking about benefit audiences that have paid too much money and thus become readily uneasy if they do not believe they are getting their money's worth. The average New York audience I find to be very much alive, to be intelligent and very appreciative of what it is given. It prizes the work. New York playgoers don't yawn in your face. A lot of English audiences I think are underenthusiastic. American audiences spoil you when they like something. They stand up and scream, they clap all the way through the play. They appreciate the writing and the situation. The audiences here are not fools. The actors get a big charge from the electricity generated by American playgoers.

GIANAKARIS: Quite recently, the young Irish actor Kenneth Branagh has received a great deal of attention. Your thoughts on him as a man of the theater?

SHAFFER: I've seen him play Touchstone; he's very clever, because that is an impossible part—perhaps the worst part in Shakespeare. Those awful jokes; humor changes, making such jokes as Touchstone's very hard to animate. Shakespeare is my god, and I worship him. But I do think his clowns are very hard to take now, almost all of them.

I think it was very bold of Branagh to do *Henry V* as a film—a very good film, incidentally. Obviously, the way Olivier spoke the great speeches is infinitely finer, grander, and more thrilling than the way Mr. Branagh does them. But that's no reason *Henry V* shouldn't be done. I admire Mr. Branagh for doing it; he obviously will arouse hostility for doing it from people who can't bear to see any ambition or any success—which is a typical attitude in England today, I'm afraid. But it isn't saying anything new to point out that Olivier was touched by genius.

GIANAKARIS: What sticks in your mind most prominently about Sir Laurence Olivier?

SHAFFER: His greatness—the compelling greatness of his performances. I saw most of them on stage when I was a young man. I saw those great seasons of what then was called the New Theatre in London. I saw his *Oedipus Rex* and *The Critic*. He surprised one all the time in most amazing ways. Kenneth Tynan once wrote that people attend the theater finally to be surprised. Olivier's *Richard III* on stage was superb and terrifying. It lost a certain amount of its terror in the movie version where it became a little too jolly and slightly camp— qualities which on stage it certainly was not. I remember Olivier as Edgar in Strindberg's *Dance of Death*. The way Larry began the play made evident all the sarcasm of the situation. Blissful married evenings would come to a conclusion. I can tell you that the audiences could see the play in some deep way, so that the last thing they would want is to be in that room with that man Edgar.

Olivier's power was enormous. And he worked to generate it. His *Othello* which was frequently mocked in this country because of the strange accent he used for the role nevertheless emitted great power. I saw the opening night of his *Othello*, and I've never forgotten it—the astounding way in which he summoned all his psychic energy. He was my idol when I was young, because he was never the same twice; he created a different electricity each time you watched him live. There was no substitute for watching him live on stage.

It seems to me that actors try to live in the flesh in front of you and are responsible for their own performances. They must authenticate the role they are playing and keep it going; they need to be aware of its structure, its architecture. Consequently, I don't know how in making movies they can submit to having it all chopped up and orchestrated for them by a director. In the movie house you are watching a director's performance just as much as an actor's.

In a way, the director in films makes the actor as well—Kazan's Brando, Forman's Murray Abraham, or Forman's Tom Hulce. Those actors are very accomplished and adroit, but what is finally shown on the screen is what the director has decided to show. He can bump up a voice or take it down. Or take the camera focus away from any given actor in a way not possible on a live stage. Movie-making is a different art, a different craft, and one I find less interesting. I like watching live people performing. That is what is fascinating about Maggie Smith in New York at this moment. People attending *Lettice & Lovage* can't believe their eyes.

GIANAKARIS: You have mentioned a new one-woman radio drama entitled *Whom Do I Have the Honour of Addressing?* What can you say about it?

SHAFFER: It was written originally for Maggie Smith during the time of her incapacitation when she had lost the use of her arm. She also had a thyroid condition, as I mentioned, so that she couldn't do television at the time. She was holed up in the country, and I figured that I might be able to write something she could do; that meant something for the radio. And I did write the play for her, but she couldn't do it anyway, because she was being operated on for her eyes. I then asked the splendid actress Judi Dench who said she would love to do the part. She ended up doing it [in May of 1989, over BBC radio], and she did it wonderfully.

I would like to do it on the stage now. It's possible to stage on television, too—in fact, it would make an effective television drama. I haven't decided yet what my next step will be with the script [scheduled for publication in 1990 by André Deutsch publishers], but I would prefer the stage since it would be more fun. On the BBC broadcast, by the way, the piece ran between 70 to 75 minutes.

GIANAKARIS: What else is in the offing?

SHAFFER: Right now I am completing what I call my "Greek Play," which is a long three-act work. The first two acts are done, and I am polishing the third one now. It's difficult and exhausting, but I must finish it. Yes, this is the same piece of which I spoke several years ago. The play somewhat resembles a fugue in that three related "plays" take place simultaneously—one concerning a playwright and his wife, one enacting the play being written by the dramatist, and one involving the wife and the son after the playwright's death. So, as you can see, it is a complicated business but one very nearly completed.

GIANAKARIS: Finally, there is a natural interest among the theatergoing public concerning your brothers. Your twin brother Anthony, also a Tony winner for his stage thriller *Sleuth,* has not been heard from recently.

SHAFFER: Tony (Anthony) has been living in Australia, writing movie scripts for what have become fairly successful films. We do keep in touch, and he informs me that he has completed a new play. Brian, my younger brother, remains an artist and a businessman in England.

EDITOR'S POSTSCRIPT: During the above conversations between C. J. Gianakaris and Peter Shaffer, the playwright received a telephone call from London giving the news of director John Dexter's death that day. Besides again insisting that Dexter was a major force in the success of many of his earlier plays [*Royal Hunt of the Sun, Black Comedy*, and *Equus*], Shaffer unreservedly deemed Dexter one of the finest directors—if not the very best director—of his time. Subsequently,

Shaffer served as spokesman concerning Dexter's life and death for the extensive coverage accorded them in *The New York Times* in the days immediately following the death.

# PETER SHAFFER'S *FIVE FINGER EXERCISE* AND THE CONVENTIONS OF REALISM

## Charles R. Lyons

As a movement within the newly international avant-garde, dramatic realism constituted a relatively brief moment of experimentation that had exhausted its novelty by the time Henrik Ibsen was writing his final sequence of plays in the eighteen-nineties.[1] Ibsen's writing, of course, participates in the complex histories of both the realistic project of the final decades of the ninteenth century and the symbolist theater of the early twentieth century. His plays were produced by those who celebrated realism and also by those who searched for theatrical modes that would supplant realism's replication of the literal. The rapid appropriation of several of Ibsen's realistic texts by those interested in a theater of images demonstrates the brevity of realism's hold on the experimental art theater.

In fact, Ibsen's texts became the vehicles for symbolist reconstruction as early as Aurelien Lugné-Poe's production of *Rosmersholm* for the Théâtre de l'Oeuvre in 1894. This performance displayed both the regisseur's defection from the realist ideology of Antoine's Théâtre Libre and the play's vulnerability to the symbolist program. By 1906, *Ghosts*, the very text that had set the course for Brahm's Freie Buhne in Berlin and Grein's Independent Theatre Society in London, had been recast by Max Reinhart in an anti-realist production designed by the Expressionist painter and graphic artist Edvard Munch. Edward Gordon Craig's production of *Rosmersholm* in 1906 with Duse as Rebekka West configured Ibsen's realistic description of the rooms of Rosmersholm into an atmospheric environment dominated by the window that looks out toward the millrace, the site of Beate's suicide and the impending marriage/suicide of Rebekka and Rosmer. After abstracting the playwright's representation of space, Craig found no great disparity between his symbolist interests and Ibsen's text. In the same year, the Meyerhold production of *Hedda Gabler* at the Theatre of Vera Komisarjevskaya ignored the detailed textual description of the Falk Villa in Ibsen's text and presented a sea-green atmosphere dominated by a large tapestry depicting a woman in silver and green.[2] Meyerhold's production documented his defection from the aesthetic of Stanislavski and the Moscow Art Theater as dynamically as Lugné-Poe's *Rosmersholm* defined his differences from Antoine.

The radical experimental theater of the early twentieth century either rejected the realistic text as irrelevant or foregrounded the imagistic structure of those plays it could reconfigure. Ironically, the commercial or mainstream theater—against which the avant-garde realism of the eighteen-eighties had defined itself—rapidly absorbed the conventions of realism. The functional principles of realism, developed in Ibsen's texts of the eighteen-eighties, continue to be exercised by popular theater, film, and television at the end of this century, despite the fact that the avant-garde abandoned its strict adherence to them by the beginning of this century. In fact, the premises associated with realism found advocates on world stages throughout all the 1900s.

Peter Shaffer's initial success in the theater, as one example, came with the 1958 London production of *Five Finger Exercise*. John Gielgud directed both this première and the American production which opened in New York a year later. The success of Shaffer's debut piece in the West End and on Broadway demonstrates the tenacity of realism as a dominant mode in those two venues of the commercial theater. Of course, 1958 marks a significant moment in the history of the contemporary theater, particularly in Britain. Recall that in 1956 John Osborne's *Look Back in Anger* initiated a movement that displaced the middle-class from the stage and displayed the interests and concerns of the underclass. While Osborne's play also relates to dramatic realism, its focus upon a proletarian hero violated the essential bourgeois concerns of traditional realism. And in *The Entertainer*, which followed in 1957, Osborne opened the realistic structure to include new musical numbers that demonstrated Archie's mediocrity as a performer. Such an inclusion energized the performance with a quasi-Brechtian thematic punctuation even though the songs were more naturalized in Osborne's shift from the dialogue of the episodes to the framed performances of the music hall than in its epic prototypes. In the same year, Roger Blin's production of *Fin de partie*, the French text that would become *Endgame* in Beckett's translation, received its first performance at the Royal Court, where Osborne's first play had been staged.[3] A year later, George Devine produced the English version at the Royal Court. The première of Harold Pinter's *The Birthday Party*—the powerful and enigmatic dramatic work that self-consciously responds to Beckett's influence—also took place in 1957. In this same time frame, the Berliner Ensemble made its historic visits to London, displaying the techniques of the Brechtian theater that would soon be answered in the writing of Osborne and Arden, as well as in the theatricality of Joan Littlewood and in the dynamic changes in Shakespearean production at the R.S.C.

As the British theater assimilated the theatrical strategies of Brecht, Beckett, and the political writings of its own theatrical left, the aesthetic arena in which Shaffer operated demanded a different kind of playwriting, one that accommodated the more innovative structures of the theatrical revolution of the late nineteen-fifties and early sixties. *Five Finger Exercise*, looking back toward the conventions of dramatic realism, respresents a type of dramatic structure that Shaffer would soon abandon as he responded more eclectically to the diverse interests of the British theater in the next three decades.[4] Re-addressing *Five Finger Exercise* in 1990, however, allows us to see its use of late nineteenth-century modes of representation and, correspondingly, to bring the conventionality of its form of realism to the foreground.

Frequently the development of modern realism has been discussed as a form of representation that eliminates convention in the suppression of the presentational strategies of episodic structure and the conscious rejection of the techniques of revealing character through soliloquy or aside.[5] The realistic theater of Ibsen, Chekhov, and Strindberg appropriated the self-interpreting scene of the realistic novel, which, ironically, imitated the objectivity of dramatic presentation.[6] Rather than analyzing the absence of a choric presence that would comment upon the dramatized action, we often have treated this apparent objectivity as an absence of convention itself rather than as a substitution of one set of artifices for another.

One of the theoretical problems of discussing realism as a mode of representation involves the implications of the term itself. That is, too frequently we accept the writer's claim that the form itself is a medium through which we perceive the *real*, that the texts function as a kind of transparency that gives us direct access to a *truthful* replication of some objective presence in the world. As we discuss the aesthetic phenomenon of realism in the theater, we need to recognize that the object of imitation is a fictional presence that is conceptualized or mediated in the notion *reality*. That is, we need to remind ourselves that it is impossible to conceptualize a set of assumptions about the world as an object of thought or a set of objectivities that is free from ideology. In other words, we need to recognize that the term *reality* makes reference to a set of conceptualizations that are, in themselves, already mediated through explicit and implicit assumptions. Realism, as a theatrical mode of presentation, implements a series of artifices and is no more aligned with the *real* than any other form of art. *Realism* does, of course, disclose the terms in which certain writers in the late nineteenth century formulated their mediation of the world of nature and human experience. However, the same statement applies to the anti-realistic mediations of Brecht, Beckett, and Pinter.

The initial response to Shaffer's first play for the theater (he had written earlier works for radio and television) included statements that identified its "truthfulness." Frederick Brisson, for example, in the preface to the American edition writes: "The play had perfect identification for my wife [the actress Rosalind Russell] and me, two Americans in a British audience. We could understand the gruff father, the culture-loving overpossessive mother, the mixed-up young son, the lonely tutor, the exuberant young girl."[7] Brisson, of course, assumes that the objective correlatives of these characters exist primarily as typical or representative figures in the experience of himself, his wife, and the playwright. In 1982, in his retrospective discussion of the play (in the *Collected Plays of Peter Shaffer*), the playwright himself posited a relationship between the text and his own biography: "Unquestionably

it expressed a great deal of my own family tensions and also a desperate
need to stop feeling invisible."[8]

While I would not deny either the "truthfulness" of the
characters, as they relate to Brisson's experience, or the playwright's
correlation between the concerns of this play and Shaffer's biography, it
is clear to me that these aspects of the content of the play shape
themselves within the highly conventionalized schemes of dramatic
realism, forms that operate within aesthetic parameters as strictly
followed as the Vice in medieval drama or as formalized as Molière's
transformations of the figures of the *commedia*. That is, while the play
may provoke its audiences and its playwright to draw alignments
between its content and their experience, it is—on one level at least—a
highly skillful manipulation of theatrical conventions that owes at least
as much to the playwright's experience of dramatic literature, in reading
and performance, as to his experience outside the theater. Responding
either deliberately or inadvertantly to the play's title, Brisson remarks:
"It is like a Bach piano piece: seemingly simple, yet interwoven and
enormously complicated" (6). My essay in this collection addresses the
play as a composition—as a facilely constructed artifice that brings
many of the fundamental conventions of late nineteenth-century realism
and its later variants into play. My objective is to understand more fully
the organizational principles operative in the text and, as well, to work
toward a clearer sense of dramatic realism itself as a theatrical artifice.
My focus therefore will be upon a series of dramatic strategies from
dramatic realism that I find operative in *Five Finger Exercise*.

Shaffer's play follows the Ibsenian model in which the nature of
the present is explained and is made plausible through the sequential
release of data about the past. Clearly the scientific model informs late
nineteenth-century dramatic realism through its implementation of
notions of determinism. Here, of course, two demands of dramatic
realism conflict. Ibsen's texts, challenging the scenography of the
theater he found in provincial Norway, demanded a three-dimensional,
functional construction of highly specific rooms, filled with real
furniture and objects. These demands limited the number of spaces
represented and required that the time span of the dramas be restricted to
the "plausible" series of moments that would occur in the room or
rooms represented. This spatial restriction, aligned with the

corresponding temporal limitation, necessitated a unity of place and time that compressed an extended narrative structure—displaying an interplay of cause and effect—into a relatively brief moment. This restriction of time and space occasions a sharp focus on the immediate present and therefore complicates the larger project of realism, the explication of cause: the documentation of the processes of time working through the determinants of biology, psychology, economics, and political and social history. Consequently, the representation of the present moment needs to disclose, through dialogue, the past that has brought this specific moment to its present condition. Here the present displays itself as the consequence of the past.

To make this presentation plausible within dialogue, Ibsen and those who follow him represent the material of the past as repressed and construct the present action as coextensive with the revelation of a narrative of the past that revises the history of its characters and discloses the structure of the present. In order to energize the representation of the present as the scene of action, the revelation of the past must surprise and change the perception of some of the characters. This pressure complicates the antithetical strategy of realism: the representation of mundane events that are, in themselves, metonymic of the ordinary transactions of middle-class experience. Reference to the past impacts the dialogue. The dialogue must be organized into extended exposition and the figures who speak this fragmented narrative must be given motive to release and to receive in scenic fragments the gradually forming narrative of the past. As that story slowly reveals itself, never in chronological sequence, certain critical lacunae become apparent; and the action of the drama works toward a significant revelation of material that is supposed for the greater part of the performance.[9]

In *Five Finger Exercise* the dialogue appears to focus on the ordinary transactions of the immediate scene but actually provides the mediated images of the past that naturalize the present alienation of the five dramatic figures that Shaffer assembles on a stage configured to resemble a stylishly decorated Suffolk country house. Louise, who presents herself as a member of the haute-bourgeoisie, the daughter of a French mother and English father, is in an estranged relationship with Stanley, her lower class husband who has made a financial success of his popular line of furniture. She sees herself as the victim of an arranged marriage, approved by her parents who sacrifice class interests for financial security. The surface complicity of Louise and Clive exploits the hostility between the teen-aged son Clive and his father who perceives the boy's interest in art and literature as the mark of deficient virility. The emerging adolescence of the young daughter Pamela and her attraction to the external social world suggests an alienation from her family that will escalate in the immediate future.

The retrospective dialogue traces the history of the initial relationship of the parents and the more recent detachment of the children. This conversion also identifies the significant lacuna that focuses on Pamela's tutor, the mystery of Walter Langer's exile from Germany that eventually discloses itself as his alienation from his Nazi father in an Oedipal paradigm that matches the one dramatized. The immediate collision of these histories determines the crisis of the present, dramatized in a limited time period, but the dynamics of these inter-relationships, to be plausible, must be seen as the phenomena of an extended history to make these figures correspond to the psychological teleologies in which realism operates.

Realism attempts to ground its characters in the specifics of a socio-economic hierarchy that reveals the exploitative aspects of capitalism. Ibsen's treatment of middle-class economic values in *A Doll's House, An Enemy of the People,* and *John Gabriel Borkman* exemplifies that conventional social judgment. Even Halvard Solness's economic success falls victim to the realist critique that aligns the interests of capitalism with the hypocrisy of middle-class morality. In Chekhov, Treplev questions the quest for popular and financial success of both Arkadina and Trigorin, and the relentless proletarian invasion of the household in *The Three Sisters* and Lopakhin's appropriation of the cherry orchard in the final play balance the proletariat and the upper-class in a mediation that reveals the necessity of the pragmatic and the pathos of loss of the aristocratic culture. Even in *Long Day's Journey into Night*, Tyrone's commercial success becomes a kind of corruption that biases his own self-judgment and the perception of his family. *A Streetcar Named Desire* mourns the loss of the aesthetic refinement that marks the disintegration of the Dubois family, indicated by both poverty and the marriage of Stella to Stanley Kowalski.

Almost inevitably in realism, characters speak the language and make the coded physical gestures of a class. Often, as is the case with Stanley in Shaffer's play, the *nouveau-riche* veneer does not succeed in hiding the nature of the figure who arrives at economic success with the perception and behavior of the underclass. One of the more subtle yet pervasive conventions of realism is the typicality of the situation in which the female of a sexual pair is from a higher social class than the male. Several well-known cases quickly come to mind. In *The Master Builder*, Aline's family estate was developed by Halvard Solness, who came into their marriage with no financial resources and built his economic success by exploiting the property of her family. *Hedda Gabler* involves a refined young woman, a general's daughter, who because of the lack of money is forced into marriage with the middle-class Tesman. Lyuboff Ranevskaya, who in *The Cherry Orchard* "married a lawyer, not a nobleman and behaved herself . . . not very virtuously," heads a family in economic decline. In *Long Day's Journey into Night* the convent-educated, upper middle-class Mary Tyrone is married to the uneducated, self-made actor James Tyrone who does not share the values of her class. *The Glass Menagerie* features Amanda Wingfield who recites her litany of wealthy and elegant suitors yet who has been deserted by the working-class husband she chose. In *A Streetcar Named Desire*, Stella Dubois is married to the lower-class factory worker Stanley Kowalski. Among even more recent dramas, there is the example of Alison, married to Jimmy Porter in *Look Back in Anger*, whose speech, values, and gestures differentiate her from the proletarian hero Jimmy.

Peter Shaffer exercises the coordinates of this recognizable paradigm in *Five Finger Exercise*. Louise, like many of her predecessors, views herself as a victim of a misalliance, mythologizes the superior position of her family, and valorizes her refinement and sensitivity by differentiating her interests and behavior from the cruder behavior of her husband. She even uses this difference as rationalization for her barely suppressed seduction of the young tutor. At the same time, this play "characterizes" Stanley as a figure who has made his own life from the natural resources of intelligence, drive, and energy. In this sense, Shaffer's play uses the conventional representation of the virility of the lower class in contrast to the emasculated, effete upper class. Here Shaffer's text infuses the characters with the kind of ambiguity that we find in Chekhov. Stanley, like Lopakhin, lacks the grace and sensitivity of the more aesthetic Louise, Clive, and Walter; but his masculine energy, while crude, accomplishes things. This identification of the aesthetic or intellectual with an ineffectual but refined graciousness in contrast to an animalistic but virile energy becomes a dominant antithesis in the realistic plays of Tennessee Williams. An obvious example is the contrast between the homosexual poet, Blanche's suicidal husband, and the aggressive masculinity of Kowalski. That opposition too informs the differentiation between the exploitative sexuality of Trigorin and the sexual ineffectuality of Treplev.

In Shaffer's drama, this conflation of class and sexuality informs the alienation between Stanley and his "aesthetic" son Clive. At the beginning of the second act, Stanley confronts Clive with his manager's report that Clive spoke of the furniture he manufactures as "shoddy and vulgar . . . [and] grotesque." Louise justifies Clive's statement by asserting to Stanley, "Just because you've got no taste, it doesn't mean we all have to follow suit" (22). Clive's complicity with his mother does not, however, blind him; and he discusses with Walter the fact that she inflates the status of his French grandparents:

> My great-grandpa, despite any impression to the contrary, did not actually grant humble petitions from his bedside:—merely industrial patents from a run-down office near the Louvre. The salary was so small that the family would have died of starvation if Hélène, my grandmother, hadn't met an English solicitor—on a cycling tour of the Loire—married him, and exchanged Brunoy for Bournemouth. Let us therefore not gasp too excitedly at the loftiness of Mother's family tree. Unbeknownst to Father, it has, you see, roots of clay. (32)

While the class disparity between Louise and Stanley exists, its gap is widened in Louise's self-narrative. As the language of the play reveals, her cultural sensibility focuses upon externals and, in several instances, she shows her ignorance of both music and literature. Her interest in culture constitutes a pose more than an animating energy.

In several "realistic" dramas, the child produced by the socio-economic misalliance is sacrificed. The revealed past of *The Master Builder* includes the story of the infant sons who died after the fire destroyed Aline's family home, the incident on which Solness re-builds his career. The drowning of Lyuboff's son Grisha is marked in the narrative disclosure of the past in *The Cherry Orchard* as the beginning of a series of retributive incidents that ends in the loss of the family estate. In *The Sea Gull*, Treplev, whose suicide ends the drama, is identified by his mother as a bourgeois, a "Kiev burgher," like his absent, undiscussed father. In *Long Day's Journey into Night* the narrative dialogue relates the death of the child Eugene with the parsimony of James Tyrone, and the text intensifies the threat of tuberculosis suffered by the younger of the two remaining sons by articulating the family's fear that Tyrone's cheapness will keep him in an inadequate sanitarium. In *The Glass Menagerie* the female child of the Wingfield misalliance, Laura, is maimed, and the alienated son, Tom, deserts his mother and sister. In *Look Back in Anger*, Alison Porter loses her unborn child, and that miscarriage destroys the possibility of further pregnancies. In Shaffer's play this sacrifice is displaced, transferred from the son, Clive, to the visitor, Walter, whose failed suicide closes the drama.

Shaffer's play uses the repetition of a musical phrase, indicating the stuck needle of Walter's phonograph, instead of the conventional gun shot that Chekhov employs in *The Sea Gull* and parodies in *Uncle Vanya*. Walter's failed suicide, however, provides a variant on the suicides that mark the end of *The Sea Gull, Hedda Gabler, Rosmersholm, The Wild Duck,* and *Miss Julie*. Each of these suicides manifests the child's inability to reconcile the desires of the self with the dominating image of a parent. Treplev ends his life unable to resolve his relationship with Arkadina; Hedda shoots herself with her father's dueling pistol, no longer able to enact her role of the General's daughter; Johannes Rosmer moves toward the suicide which he calls a marriage with Rebekka, incorporating the religious and military ethic of his family in his own self-judgment; Rebekka joins him, in part acting out the guilt she feels having learned that she herself is guilty of incest since her adoptive father with whom she had an earlier sexual relationship was her natural father; Hedvig shoots herself as a sacrifice to prove her love for her adoptive father; Julie convinces her father's servant to kill her, removing herself from the judgment of her father.

In parallel fashion, Walter—discovering the psychological destructiveness of the family he wishes to make his own—attempts to kill himself when they expel him from their circle. Unable to accommodate the fact of his Nazi father and his mother's acceptance of his father's evil, Walter attempts to substitute the Harrington family for his own. Damaged further by this family, he elects death. The child, injured by the psychological, the repressed ideology, or the exploitative ethic of the parent constitutes a regular figure in modern realistic drama, and the physical sacrifice of that figure often ends the play. Thus, in *Five Finger Exercise* Shaffer follows familiar footsteps in dramatic realism to bring his play to a close. Shaffer abrogates the potential melodrama of this ending, however, by representing Walter's suicide a failure, providing the opportunity for Clive's prayer for "courage" as the curtain falls.

A disruptive sexual transgression informs the conventional content of most realistic drama. Numerous examples exist of the pattern: the sexual behavior that caused Captain Alving's syphilis and the potentially incentuous relationship of Oswald and Regina; the erotic encounter ten years earlier between the middle-aged Solness and the pre-adolescent Hilde that forms a titillating narrative prelude to the eroticism of their current relationship; Arkadina's sexual relationship with Trigorin which, after permitting his seduction of Nina, resumes when that liaison ends; the eroticism of Lyuboff's young lover whose appeal calls her back to Paris; the whoring of Jamie Tyrone who initiates Edmund into the kind of debauchery that is destroying his life; the "inevitable" sexual encounter between Blanche and Stanley Kowalski; Jimmy Porter's liaison with Helena as well as the blatantly sexual basis of his relationship with Alison.

In *Five Finger Exercise* the transgressive nature of Louise's sexual attraction to Walter Langer, the twenty-two-year-old German "boy" whom she has hired as tutor to her daughter, provides the overt energy that drives the plot. This attraction, of course, relates to the conventional function of the external agent whose presence operates as a catalyst bringing the essential conflicts to the surface. Similar instances involve Trigorin in *The Sea Gull*, Lopakhin in *The Cherry Orchard*, Hilde Wangel in *The Master Builder*, the Gentleman Caller in *The Glass Menagerie*, and Helena in *Look Back in Anger*. The presence of Walter Langer, curiously the erotic center of attraction in this text, stimulates the sexuality of Louise (who clearly is estranged from her husband), attracts the nascent sexuality of the fourteen-year-old Pamela, and activates the latent homosexuality of the nineteen-year-old Clive.

In the late nineteenth century, realistic drama placed sexual transgression on the stage in texts that became notorious. For example, Ibsen's representation of Captain Alving's sexuality, venereal disease, Regina's illegitimacy, and the possibility of an incestuous relationship between Oswald and Regina violated the received expectations of the subject matter appropriate to the theater. However, while the material of these texts extended the limits of what was allowed in the theater, their dialogue operated within rules that restricted references to sexuality, perversity, and disease to the masked language of subtle circumlocution. Though the stage of 1958 was subject to a level of censorship stricter than was the theater of the 1980s, this moment was freer to identify sexual practices by direct names than the more indirect language of its nineteenth-century prototype. And yet the sexual dynamics of *Five Finger Exercise* operate under the surface of its language, both through its characters' careful circumlocution and through a series of careful substitutions.

First of all, the presence of the German tutor, as mentioned earlier, clarifies or brings to the surface repressed sexual desires. Shaffer's text displays Pamela's erotic interest in Walter at several points. In the first scene of the first act, she accompanies her verbal play, which instructs him to assume a romantic role, by smoothing back his hair and then ruffling it as he rejects her physical contact. At the end of the second scene of the same act, she appears before him in her nightgown and then comments on his embarrassment after flaunting her "indiscretion."

In Louise's language, Walter's intellectual and aesthetic interests correlate with his physical characteristics: ". . . such delicate hands . . . and that fair hair—. . . the hair of a poet." In that sense, he forms a slightly more mature version of the aesthetic and intellectual son. The text formulates this image as a counterpart to Clive that replicates or substitutes for the son. The text positions Louise's attraction toward him as a kind of incest, both in this substitution and in that critical moment in which Louise misinterprets his interests in her and is deflated by his intention that she function as a kind of mother for him:

> LOUISE:      . . . Dear little owl. . . . What's the matter
> . . . ? Are you embarrassed?
> [*He shakes his head "No."* ]
> It's the last thing you must ever be with me.
> [WALTER *smiles.*]
> What are you thinking? Come on: tell me.
> WALTER:   Some things grow more when they are not
> talked about.
> LOUISE:    Try, anyway. I want you to.
> WALTER    [*Looking away from her*]: It is only that you
> have made me wonder—
> LOUISE    [*Prompting eagerly*]: Tell me.
> WALTER    [*Lowering his voice still more*]; Mrs.
> Harrington, forgive me for asking this, but
> do you think it's possible for someone to
> find a new mother?
> [LOUISE *sits very still. The expression of eagerness
> fades, and its remnant hardens on her face. She stares at
> him.*] (54–55)

During the first episode in which Louise subtly explores her relationship with Walter, Clive enters and for a moment watches the intimate scene between the two, filling in its surface circumlocution with an intuitive understanding of the erotic content, at least on his mother's part. As Clive enters the room, Louise has just taken Walter's head in her hands and drawn it close to her. Touching the young German boy's blonde head seems to function in Shaffer's text as a signal of his erotic appeal and the desire of those who caress his hair. When Clive repeats the incident to his father, he improvises upon this perceived eroticism and extends its transgressive nature: "There on the sofa. I saw them. I came in and there they were. The light was turned down. They were kissing. *Kissing!* She was half undressed, and he was kissing her, on the mouth. On the breasts. Kissing. . ." (39). If Clive had not interrupted the scene, Louise would have learned that Walter's interest in her was not sexual in the sense she interprets. Clive's extrapolation, which functions as a kind of fantasy, voices his jealousy of the tutor and, at the same time, his own desire to be in Walter's role, the direct object of his mother's erotic energy. Clive's elaboration of this incident seems to represent his own sexual ambivalence; that is, he seems to identify with Walter and with his mother in casting himself both in the role of Walter as subject, making love to his mother, and, as the scene later clarifies, identifying with his mother as the object of Clive's sexual interest.

In between witnessing this scene and amplifying it in his report to his father, Clive moves into a dialogue with Walter that does not seem to be directly informed with jealousy of the tutor. Curiously, he expresses his attraction for the German youth in the same gesture that Pamela and his mother use:

> CLIVE *goes slowly over to* WALTER *and fingers his dishevelled hair. He is evidently fairly drunk, but alcohol does not impair his speech. Rather it gives it energy and turns of speed. Now he is more disturbed than he himself is aware.* (31)

Here he attempts two strategies, each unsuccessful. First, he attempts to warn Clive that the tutor's vision of the family structure is naively incorrect: "And believe me, love, sooner or later, like any valuable possession, you will be used. I know this family, let me tell you. If you can't help one of us score a point over the others—you've no claim on our notice" (50). Second, he attempts to effect his own indirect seduction of Walter, inviting him to become his friend and go away with him for a holiday:

| CLIVE: | . . . [*with sudden animation.*] Come away with me. |
|---|---|
| WALTER | [*Startled* ]: What? Come away? |
| CLIVE: | Look—in four weeks my term ends. We could go somewhere; to the West Country, if you like. Wells Cathedral is the most astonishing thing in England. It's like |

> walking down the throat of a whale: a
> skeleton whale, with the vertebrae showing.
> No one will be there at Christmas. (34)

Shaffer embeds the implicit eroticism of this invitation in the image of entering Wells Cathedral as the penetration of a womb, shared as a holiday adventure—private—while everyone else is celebrating.

While *Five Finger Exercise* occasionally conflates the characters of Walter and Clive so that Walter functions as a kind of substitute for the son in the play's self-conscious use of an Oedipal triangle, the text also differentiates between them. Walter's narrative recitation of his sexual encounter with the girl in the grocery shop in Muhlbach has the ostensible purpose of convincing Clive of the unimportance of sexual experience in the process of growing up; and yet its placement in this dialogue suggests a rather gratuitous clarification of Walter's heterosexuality and works to suppress the potential homoeroticism of the relationship between the two young men—a suppression accomplished in a typical late-nineteenth-century circumlocution. Continuing the reinforcement of that insistence, the dialogue between the young men foregrounds the conventional heterosexuality of Walter's desire for the future and, by the neutrality of its language, subtly suggests the repressed homosexuality in Clive's hopes:

> WALTER:   . . . I could tell you what *I* want. . . . To live
> in England. To be happy teaching. One day
> to marry. To have children, and many
> English friends. . . . And now you. What do
> *you* want?
>
> [*Pause.*]
> CLIVE       [*Faintly*]: Something—I'm not sure.
> [*Intimately.*] Yes—I think I want . . . to
> achieve something that only I could do. I
> want to fall in love with just one person. To
> know what it is to bless and be blessed. And
> to serve a great cause with devotion.
> [*Appealing.*] I want to be *involved.* (65)

Part of the power of this play in performance derives from the tension manifested in the suppression of its content: the repressed incest and homoeroticism.

*Five Finger Exercise* is, certainly, a highly conventional and derivative text that attempts to address the domestic and social issues of its moment with originality at the same time that it exploits, with varying success, the conventions of late-nineteenth-century realism. The deferred revelation of Walter's motive for leaving Germany, for example, aligns structurally with the Oedipal triangle of his substitute family, reinforcing the image of the son alienated from a brutish father; but—as the formulaic revealed secret—this disclosure provides an inadequate surprise that doesn't really inform and alter the present condition of this structure of human relations. The play does, however, manifest the playwright's skill in providing arresting theatrical images and, even more clearly, his ability to write dialogue that readily offers a sense of individualized dramatic figures. At the same time, Shaffer's dialogue embodies the kind of wit that amplifies the delight of *Amadeus* and supplies the material for the rich pleasures of Maggie Smith's performance in *Lettice and Lovage*.

# Notes

1. Ibsen's experimentation in the realistic, which perhaps begins in the prose dialogue of the epic-scaled *Emperor and Galilean*, found its fundamental structural organization in *Pillars of the Community* in 1877. While that organization remains intact through *When We Dead Awaken* in 1899, the final series of plays does loosen that form. Strindberg's appropriation of realism, most articulately defined in his preface to *Miss Julie* in 1888 and realized in the text itself, was displaced in 1898 by the proto-expressionism of *To Damascus* and *The Dream Play* in 1906 and of *The Ghost Sonata* in 1907. Chekhov's final plays, of course, which stand in between the realist project and emerging symbolism, extend from 1896 to 1904.

2. Ibsen's reputation as a realist, particularly as a realist involved in liberalism's attack on European capitalism, survived the theater's reformation of his texts in the practices of symbolism. However, the symbolist theater's emphasis upon the imagery of the plays—reinforced in an anti-realistic scenography—anticipated the directions that Ibsen scholarship would follow a few decades later.

3. Recall that, despite the fact of the success of *En attendant Godot*, Beckett and Blin were unable to find a theater for *Fin de partie* and arranged its première at the Royal Court, creating the ironic situation of a play in French, written by an Irishman, performed by French actors for an English-speaking audience.

4. It is interesting to speculate about the kind of play that Shaffer would have written, concentrating upon this same material, only a few years later. Consider for example Albee's use of some of the same conventions in *Who's Afraid of Virginia Woolf?* To push the analogy further: consider Sam Shepard's treatment of the same familial paradigms in *Buried Child* in 1977.

5. Shaffer assumes that the objective of the carefully "wrought" text is to conceal its conventionality. In the preface to his collected plays, he states, "if a play irritates by seeming to be too well made, this surely means that it has not been well made enough: that the smoothness of the joinery is sealing the work off from the viewer" (*The Collected Plays of Peter Shaffer* [New York: Harmony Books, 1982], p. xiii).

6. Recall James Joyce's assertion of the value of using the self-interpreting, objective form of dramatic writing for the novel in that passage in *The Portrait of an Artist as a Young Man* in which he compares the novelist with the detached figure of God, "paring his fingernails." Joyce, of course, venerated Ibsen's playwriting, and even learned Norwegian to read his master in the original language. The first published writing by the eighteen-year-old Joyce was his essay on a production of *When We Dead Awaken*.

7. Frederick Brisson, "Preface," Peter Shaffer, *Five Finger Exercise* (New York: Harcourt, Brace and Company, 1958), p. 5.

8. Peter Shaffer, *The Collected Plays of Peter Shaffer* (New York: Harmony Books, 1982), p. 6. The quotations from *Five Finger Exercise* used are identified in the text with page reference to this edition.

9. Ibsen of course does not invent this conventional structure; the form has its clear prototype in the organizational pattern of Sophocles'

*Oedipus* in which the complex narrative fragments of oracle, intended infanticide, parricide, and incest are naturalized in the immediate need to identify and punish the criminal whose action has polluted the polis and necessitated the plague.

# "KNOW THYSELF": INTEGRITY AND SELF-AWARENESS IN THE EARLY PLAYS OF PETER SHAFFER

## Gene A. Plunka

During the late 1950s and early 1960s, Peter Shaffer—who had worked as a salesman, library acquisitions agent, real estate clerk in his father's business office, music publishing cataloguer, music critic, novelist, and television/radio script writer—was desperately seeking an identity of his own. In the preface to *The Collected Plays of Peter Shaffer*, he explained the dilemma confronting him during this period of his life: "A frustrated fellow in my twenties, I went on believing that what I enjoyed doing—writing—was frivolous, and what bored me completely—commerce—was serious."[1] The young Shaffer was cowed into accepting the popular stance that business represented reality and art was merely pretense. Despite such dubious advice from family and friends, Shaffer made the leap from business lackey to successful playwright by ignoring egregious counsel while being true to his own needs and desires. This concept of the divided self, which unfolds into the dialect between the Apollonian and Dionysian in later plays, reflects the tension that is at the core of Shaffer's first three plays: *Five Finger Exercise, The Private Ear*, and *The Public Eye*. In these works, written between 1958 and 1962, Shaffer depicts the conflict between logic and instinct, which culminates in a plea for the individual to follow his own values, free from the advice and harangues of others.

Shaffer has stated that his first play, *Five Finger Exercise* (1958), is concerned with how individuals often are not allowed to follow their instincts but must conform to socially accepted mores: "It seems it's [the play] concerned with various levels of dishonesty."[2] Shaffer, identifying with young Clive whose Cambridge education made him feel "unemployable," says that the play "expressed a great deal of my own family tensions and also a desperate need to stop feeling invisible."[3] The family tensions are a result of the dishonesty that pervades the play; the Harringtons live in a world of illusion in which they refuse to accept Clive as an individual with a viable future free from their preconceived notions of how to mold their son.

Dennis A. Klein has noted, "there is not one happy marriage in all of Shaffer's plays, and the trend goes back even further than *Five Finger Exercise* to *The Prodigal Father*."[4] Gore Vidal carries this notion one step beyond, stating that Shaffer's purpose in *Five Finger Exercise* was to depict the decline of the family in Western society.[5] Joan F. Dean, who insists that the family is a vital element in Shaffer's dramas, acknowledges that by the end of his first play, the family fails to function as a unit because of their myopic individual views.[6] Although *Five Finger Exercise* has much in common with Ivan Turgenev's *A Month in the Country* and with the domestic dramas of Arthur Pinero and Terence Rattigan, its examination of individual identity in relationship to social codes of behavior extends the play beyond the ramifications of a typical "kitchen-sink" drama or farce.

The title of the play suggests a polyphonic musical composition in which the characters have equal parts—typical of many naturalistic domestic dramas. Upon closer examination, one discovers that Clive, who sticks out like the sore thumb of the "five finger exercise," is on stage more than any other character and becomes the focal point of the play. His dilemma stems from the fact that, like the young Peter Shaffer, he is forced to choose between the security of the family and the psychological need to establish his own identity free from familial restraint. In this context, Pamela's "Clive! Wake up, wake up, whoever you are!," can be construed as an exhortation for self-awareness.[7] Clive explains to Walter the paradox that obviously concerned the young Peter Shaffer: "The trouble is if you don't spend your life yourself, other people spend it for you. . . . As I see it, unless I suddenly feel a call from above, I'm going to wind up unemployable" (78). In addition, Clive is the character frantically caught in the middle of a marriage that is degenerating daily. Harangued by an affectatious mother who dotes on him and ignored by a father who refuses to understand him, Clive would like to receive more attention from his father and less from his mother. Instead, he becomes fodder in a battleground of verbal warfare: "The war you both declared when you married. The culture war with me as ammunition. 'Let's show him how small he is'—'Let's show her where she gets off'. *And always through me!* " (106).

Stanley and Louise Harrington have grown further apart as time progressed. Shaffer describes Stanley as "*a forceful man in middle age, well built and self-possessed, though there is something deeply insecure about his assertiveness*" (12). Louise initially saw her spouse as the pillar of society, a furniture salesman with practical sense who could provide a decent living for his family. Indeed, Stanley usually talks about such practical concerns as making contact in the business world, earning a living, acquiring money, or Clive's studying something "useful" at the university. He is proud to be the breadwinner of the family despite an obvious lack of a university education. With a mother who dies at childbirth and a father in the Merchant Marine, Stanley was forced to take care of himself. His pragmatism surfaces throughout the play.

Louise, on the other hand, has little interest in practical or business affairs, which she considers plebian; instead, she longs for gentility. She is described as "*a Person of Taste*" (9), with Shaffer's uncharacteristic use of capital letters suggesting homage to nobility. Her ostentatious way of dressing coincides with her preoccupation with social mobility. Shaffer implies that Louise is more closely attuned to outward appearances than she is to the emotional needs of her family: "*Her whole manner bespeaks a constant preoccupation with style, though without apparent insincerity or affectation*" (11). Mrs. Harrington seems to embrace whatever might be fashionable in high society, whether it be German poetry (which she cannot understand but insists must be beautiful because of its sound), classical music, French culture, or Greek drama (even though she often forgets the titles of specific plays). Clive bitterly asserts to Walter, "Being French, you know, Mother imagines she's real ormolu in a sitting-room of plaster gilt. She suffers from what I might call a plaster-gilt complex, if you see what I mean" (49). Her desire to partake in upper class society necessitates her choice of gallant Walter Langer as a tutor for her daughter, who must be schooled in all of the proper social graces. Louise Harrington appears to be living in a fantasy world, for although she aspires to the aristocracy, her roots are at best middle class: her grandfather was a French clerk in an industrial patents office.

Louise and Stanley Harrington are not a happy couple. Clive adequately assesses their relationship when he says, "The rift you may detect between them is the difference between the Salon and the Saloon" (49). Stanley is sarcastic about Louise's attempts to convert their Suffolk cottage into something akin to a French chateau. Stanley has little use for Louise's passion for beautiful poetry or French culture; there is no money in it for him. Louise's classical music only gives Stanley headaches. Although Stanley was never intrigued by Louise's cultural pursuits, Louise, in an attempt to salvage the marriage, admits, "I've tried to be interested in his bridge and his golf club and his terrible friends. I just can't do it. . ." (44). Her benign attempts to cajole her husband by taking an interest in Stanley's hobbies fail to assuage family tensions. Instead, Louise prefers to dictate taste to her husband. As the house decorator, she controls the environment which *"is well furnished, and almost aggressively expresses Mrs. Harrington's personality"* (9). She insists on having a tutor for Pamela, which intrudes on the delicate family structure. Clive is to matriculate at Cambridge, which she proudly reminds Stanley is "our leading University" (39). As the center of the family, she barks orders and provides advice to her acolytes, consistently urging Pamela to dress warmly (75) or take her bath (85), Stanley to come in from the cold (70), or Clive to get on with his breakfast (14). Despite her attempts to mold the family in conformance with her wishes, she leads a miserable life.

The Harringtons have drifted further apart, and their failure to communicate effectively has destroyed their marriage. Louise is candid about their hypocritical existence: "It's no good, Stanley. My life was never meant to be like this—limited this way. . ." (88). Louise concludes that her married life is unbearable: "But don't you see I'm just so frustrated I don't know what I'm doing half the time? I'm sorry, but it's the only word, Stanley. There are times I feel I'm being absolutely choked to death—suffocated under piles of English blankets" (88). To relieve this frustration, Louise turns to Walter as source of inspiration. Walter becomes the object of Louise's passion as a result of a marriage that fails to provide her with the sexual and intellectual stimulation that she craves.

Unfortunately, Clive is caught in the middle of these family tensions. Desperately seeking his own identity, Clive instead becomes a whipping boy, an ineffective sparring partner on whom his parents can vent their frustrations. His mother uses Clive as mutual support in her extended warfare with Stanley; Clive even looks like his mother, and his interest in the arts is something they both have in common. Stanley, in fact, considers his son to be a "momma's boy." Louise uses Clive to her advantage, controlling his behavior, wishing to turn him into an object for her satisfaction—a fact Clive readily grasps: "For example—my Mother's name for me—Jou-jou. Toy. More accurately in this case, ornament" (48–49). Astute Pamela perceptively views her brother as a "slave boy" (69) whose identity is subsumed by the whims of his parents. As an object or ornament in the family, Clive, Pamela suggests, "spends his whole time not being listened to" (63). Clive even compares himself to a puppy trotting faithfully alongside his parents: " 'Clive, to heel, sir. Heel!' Let me introduce myself: 'Spaniel Harrington'" (40). He views his parents as being honored members of the "absolute Power Department" (77).

Clive's self-awareness and his keen ability to perceive his inferior status in the family enables him to admonish Walter, however unsuccessfully, about the tutor's dependence on others. Clive tries to persuade Walter to refuse to be "taken up! Like a fashion. Or an ornament; a piece of Dresden, a dear little Dresden owl" (50). "Spaniel" Harrington warns Walter of the dangers of becoming the family pet: "When in hell are you going to stop trading on your helplessness—offering yourself all day to be petted and stroked?" (52). However, Walter's dilemma is the inverse of Clive's paradox: Walter seeks a family, while Clive needs to be more independent. Thus, Clive's hope of inviting Walter to share in his predicament, a sort of "misery loves company" resolution, is ineffective.

Clive's relationship with his father is quite strained. Stanley, who ideally would like to mold his son in his own image, admonishes Clive for keeping company with "arty-tarty boys" (16) and for refusing to study "useful" subjects at Cambridge University which, he laments, "your mother insists you're to go to" (16). Whereas Clive believes education is its own reward, Stanley castigates his son for refusing to recognize the importance of material goods: "Don't ever be so stupid as to look down on money. It's the one thing that counts in the end" (38). Stanley's pragmatism is lost on Clive, whose decision to study the humanities at the university places him squarely on Louise's side in the continuing familial warfare. Stanley can only resentfully state to Clive, "I just don't understand you at all" (18).

Clive will never be able to be himself until he is free from his father's authority. Shaffer describes Clive as *"quick, nervous, taut and likeable"* (11), one whose *"nervousness instinctively increases with his* [Stanley's] *appearance"* (12). Pamela tells her father that Clive could never talk to him "man to man" unless he were drunk; otherwise, Clive would be too nervous to speak his mind. In the presence of his father, Clive feels as if he is constantly being challenged and must defend his right to be a unique individual. Walter tells Stanley that Clive "does not wish to be alone with you because always he feels you are—well—judging him. When you look at him, he sees you are thinking—'How useless he is'" (93). Walter explains to Stanley how the relationship degenerated into master-slave: "You are wrong about him. You see in front of you he must always justify his life" (94). Clive's relationship with his father develops into love-hate, with Clive's need for acceptance and the concomitant refusal of his father to support his lifestyle contributing to the sense of uneasiness existing between father and son. This anxiety is expressly manifested in Clive's recurrent dream in which his father enters his son's room at night and carefully removes the ten blankets from the youngster's bed. Clive eventually wakes up shivering. His relationship with his father is therefore seen as disconcerting, cold, unnerving, and remote. Clive would rather drink alone in his room than accompany his father to the pub. He even accuses his father of driving him to drink (57).

Clive yearns to be true to himself, yet his stifling environment, one which ignores his spiritual and emotional needs, precludes growth. He regrets that his parents provide advice but no intellectual challenge: "Why doesn't a night's sleep lying all those dark hours with ourselves forgotten and then coming alive again, why doesn't it ever change us? Give us new things to see—new things to say too: not just 'Eat your eggs', or 'You were in late'—the old dreariness" (107). Clive pleads with his parents to cease treating him as an object, puppet, or ornament created in their own image. He castigates his father, who does not "even know the right way to treat a child. Because a child is private and important and *itself*, not an extension of you, any more than I am" (57). Clive argues that his inner needs are more important than the career expectations that his parents have for him: "Because what you do in the world and so on isn't important at all, not in the slightest, compared with what you look like and sound like and feel like as the minutes go by" (58). Clive reiterates, "I am myself. Myself. Myself. You think of me only as what I might become. What I might make of myself. But I am myself now—with every breath I take, every blink of the eyelash" (57). Clive's dilemma is whether to remain in the secure, safe womb of the family at the expense of losing his wits amidst the verbal warfare or to flee the "womb-tomb" as did his alter ego, Walter Langer. Speaking under his breath to Walter, Clive admits, "It's a marvellous dispensation: to escape one's inheritance" (51). Shaffer drives home his point clearly when he notes that Clive is now writing critical articles for a magazine called *New Endeavor*. The title describes Clive's break with the family—a leap into the unknown yet the only way to find his own identity.

Clive lacks suitable role models to lead him out of his stifling environment into his own independence. He admires his Indian friend at Cambridge because he is at peace with himself. Pamela also is a free spirit; she certainly is not used as cannon fodder during the family's constant battling. However, in no way can she be considered a role model for Clive, especially at her age. The young man has no female companions, "not even acquaintanceships," says Pamela (63). Because of this lack of contact, Clive implores Walter to take a vacation with him for, as Clive says, "I need a friend so badly" (52).[8] When Walter rebuffs Clive in his attempt to make contact, the German tutor explains that he enjoys fulfilling his obligation to the Harrington household and has no need to flee. Walter's needs are not Clive's, but the latter fails to comprehend this. Clive imposes his own values on Walter, urging him to leave the household "for your sake. Only for your sake, believe me. . . . You've got a crush on our family that's almost obscene. Can't you see how lucky you are to be on your own?" (78–79). Feeling rebuffed,

Clive lies to his father about Walter kissing Louise on her breasts. Ironically enough, Clive's dishonesty—coming from someone who pleaded for truth in his own family—serves to destroy another person's happiness.

Clive actually views Walter as a potential role model. Only three years older than Clive, Walter already is on his own without having to depend on his parents for support. Because of his father's activity in the Nazi party, Walter has severed all ties with his German ancestry, refuses to teach German, and hopes to acquire full English citizenship. Clive, however, is disappointed that Walter chooses to depend on anyone and warns him, "This isn't a family. It's a tribe of wild cannibals. Between us we eat everyone we can" (25). When Clive betrays Walter, Stanley makes it clear that Walter will have to return to Germany and will never be able to obtain his naturalization papers. Walter, who has a sense of morality, dignity, and responsibility, attempts suicide because everything he has worked for has been destroyed. Clive thus intuitively understands that Walter is a suitable role model, true to his own values. To Clive, Walter's attempted suicide is "The courage. For all of us" (110).

Shaffer's second play, *The Private Ear* (1962), is a one-act drama that depicts the disasters that befall individuals who imitate others instead of being true to themselves. In an interview with Barry Pree and in the preface to his collected works, Shaffer stated that he empathizes with Bob, the young man searching for his identity.[9] Bob, whose lack of a last name coincides with his identity crisis, has yet to find his true calling in life. He acknowledges that he is merely "a glorified office boy"[10] who does mundane tasks in an import-export business. He realizes that he is wasting his talents working as a clerk but fears taking the necessary steps to change his banal existence. Bob admits, "When I wake up I've got so much energy. I could write a whole book—paint great swirling pictures on the ceiling. But what am I *actually* going to do? Just fill in about five hundred invoices" (53). Like Clive who is defined by his family, Bob is a product of his enslaving work environment. He states woefully, "We weren't born to do this. Eyes. Complicated things like eyes, weren't made by God just to see columns of pounds, shillings, and pence written up in a ledger" (53). His question to Doreen about her trite job, "Are you going to spend the rest of your life being somebody else's obedient servant, original and two carbons?" (53), actually sums up *his* hapless situation.

Bob has met Doreen at a concert and mistakenly assumed that their mutual interest in music will assure some degree of compatibility between them. Unfortunately, they have little in common, something Bob should have foreseen after their initial soiree at an expresso bar in Kensington produced an evening of virtual silence. In fact, her prosaic personality is incongruous with Bob's idyllic vision of her as Botticelli's Venus. Furthermore, Bob's introverted nature and his visions of the ideal make him ill-suited for Doreen, who prefers someone more extroverted, like Ted.

Although Bob may not have foreseen such personality differences between Doreen and himself, the more significant reason for the disastrous reunion is because of Bob's inability to be true to himself. Alone with Doreen, Bob seems to do fairly well with the conversation, although he can never be considered a witty or loquacious speaker. He manages to keep the conversation flowing, especially when it relates to his passion for music, or when he makes an attempt to joke with Doreen, or to discuss his future aspirations, along the way trying to inspire Doreen to escape her nine-to-five existence; and he certainly pontificates much more than does Doreen. However, the evening is destined to be a disaster because Bob, who is insecure, does not rely on his instincts and true feelings. Instead, he has asked Ted to help out with the conversation, and Ted, who is boisterous and self-confident, puts enough pressure on Bob to ruin the evening for him.

Bob has asked his alter ego for advice and solace, but the fact that they have completely different lifestyles makes Ted an inappropriate choice as a mentor for Bob. Shaffer describes Bob as "*an awkward young man in his late teens or early twenties, and his whole manner exudes an evident lack of confidence—in himself and in life*" (13). Ted, on the other hand, is "*cocky and extroverted, fitted out gaily by Shaftesbury Avenue to match his own inner confidence and self-approval*" (13). Whereas Ted tries to be chic, Bob is depicted as a hapless working class lad from "the provinces" (16). Ted is at home with women, many of whom he meets in bars and discotheques. In contrast, Bob has never had a date before. Ted is somewhat ambitious and even studies French in his spare time; Bob is content to be a drone in the office. In addition, Ted is always cheerful and garrulous, while Bob tends to be moody and rather petulant. Finally, Ted is meticulous about his appearance, taking care to comb his hair or to dress for the ladies; Bob is more slovenly and even reveals that he has never used deodorant prior to their first date.

Despite the obvious differences between Bob and Ted, Bob's lack of self-confidence motivates him to ask Ted for advice in assuring that he has a successful evening with Doreen. Bob is uneasy about relying on Ted's prowess with women rather than on his own instincts: "That's why all that stuff is so silly—all this plotting: I say this, and she says that. I think things should just happen between people" (21). Bob is unable to be true to himself because Ted is trying to mold his friend in his own image. Before Doreen enters, Ted is coaching Bob about social mores, creating unnecessary tension before Bob's date starts: "You know what you're going to do this evening? I mean, you know what I'm expecting you to do, don't you?" (16). Ted, referring to the date as "the most important night of your life" (14), insists that Bob impress Doreen with his chic, suave lifestyle, of which Bob is totally ignorant. Ted urges Bob to reset the table properly, not realizing that Doreen is just as nervous as Bob and would probably overlook such an insignificant matter of etiquette. And Ted's insistence causes Bob to upset a vase and make a mess. Meanwhile, biting his nails, Bob waits for Doreen to enter so the two can mutually suffer through the evening.

When Doreen arrives, we realize that Bob has invited Ted "to help out with the talk" (20), and when his mentor is offstage in the kitchen, Bob tries to adopt Ted's personality. As one consequence, Bob fumbles with the cigarette lighter because he does not smoke and never has needed to use a lighter before; however, Ted had explained that lighting a cigarette in one's mouth and then handing it to your date would be quite intimate. Bob offers Doreen a glass of Dubonnet— originally Ted's idea—but sheepishly admits that he has none to offer since he does not drink. The banter becomes even more insipid as we learn that Doreen is a teetotaler too. Moreover, the dinner is further strained because of the verbal insult hurled at Ted whose derisory comments about opera have offended the normally complacent Bob.

As the evening progresses, Bob loses his identity even more and begins to sound more and more like Ted. He becomes a sort of automaton, mouthing words that he has heard Ted speak. As Bob describes his nonexistent girlfriend to Doreen, she is aware that he is lying. Bob's assessment of Lavinia, "That's really raven black, her hair. It's got tints of blue in it" (58), derives from Ted's comments about *his* girlfriend's hair: "Raven black. It's got tints of blue in it" (16). Bob's use of the word "carriage" to describe his imaginary idyllic beauty (58) parallels Ted's reference to "carriage" in a private conversation with Bob (17) and also alone with Doreen (47). Similarly, Bob's determination to spice up his vocabulary by referring to Doreen's ocelot coat as "very chic" (25) only marks him as a pale imitator of Ted, especially since Ted understands the meaning of the French words. Additionally, Bob only makes a fool of himself upon learning both that Doreen's coat is actually nylon and that ocelot is not a bird. Finally, when Bob reminds Doreen, "Alcohol's not really a stimulant at all, you know—it's a depressant" (52), Doreen exasperatingly acknowledges, "I know. I heard" (52), because Ted stated the same warning to her ten minutes earlier.

The pressure on Bob to deny his own integrity in order to assimilate Ted's personality ultimately irritates and confuses the young man. Ted's advice, "This is a girl, not a goddess. Just you give her a shove off her pedestal" (49), followed by his plea that "This is the critical moment. If you louse this up, I'm going to be very upset" (49), undermines Bob's self-awareness and rechannels his efforts to conform to Ted's wishes. Bob has relied on Ted to buy the flowers, get the wine, cook the dinner, liven the conversation, and even supply the clichés. In exchange, Bob has lost his self-respect, and he lashes out at Ted for his interference in Bob's life: "I'm just someone to look down on, aren't I? Teach tricks to. Like a bloody monkey. You're the organ grinder, and I'm the monkey! And that's the way you want people. Well—go home, Ted. Find yourself another monkey!" (50). However, Ted's departure does not lessen the pressure on Bob to behave the way his mentor had instructed him. The result is that Bob, *"his mind full of how Ted would act under these circumstances"* (56), haplessly tries to seduce Doreen. After he is slapped for his feeble effort of falling on top of her, Bob is reduced to lying as he explains to Doreen that "I've got a girl friend of my own already" (57). The disastrous evening ends as Bob deliberately scratches one of his cherished records—the culmination of his frustrations of not being in control of the situation.

Like Stanley Harrington providing advice to Clive, Ted offers social tips to Bob. Yet Bob, like Clive, can only assure his integrity by heeding his own instincts. As Charles A. Pennel notes, Bob uses pretense to camouflage his true self.[11] Bob could eventually learn on his own that Ted is more suited to Doreen; Bob's idealistic visions are not compatible with her working class virtues. Instead, Bob's reliance on Ted's diction has only served to increase his own isolation and destroy his self-confidence and integrity. Bob should have paid attention to what his idol Peter Grimes had to say to him—even a lonely man can reject the solicitude of others.[12]

*The Public Eye*, a one-act play that was written to accompany *The Private Ear*, is also concerned with the dialectic between staid logic versus spirit or inner conviction. Charles Sidley, a Bloomsbury accountant, has hired a private detective, Julian Cristoforou, to follow his wife, whom he suspects has been unfaithful in their marriage. To his chagrin Sidley learns that his fatherly advice to his young wife had stifled her freedom and has discouraged her from being true to her own values and instincts; he has as a consequence destroyed his own marriage.

Cristoforou summarizes the problem that characterizes the disintegrating marriage: "We are born living, and yet how ready we are to play possum and fake death" (112). Belinda is a free spirit, actively engaged in life's pleasures. She is described as *"a pretty young girl of twenty-two, wearing bright unconventional clothes and a green trilby"* (87). She lived the first eighteen years of her life in Northampton but rebelled against her parents' parochial goals of having her marry a local boy and then work in some trivial administrative capacity for the rest of her life. Instead, Belinda fled to London, lived with two bohemian artists, and wound up working as a waitress in the Up-to-Date Club in Soho, where she met Sidley. Although Sidley was twice her age, the marriage was successful at first because Sidley felt like a new man and now had a pupil to teach. Unfortunately, Belinda soon began to disapprove of her subservience to her new mentor, who unwisely destroyed the balance of reciprocity between them.

Like her predecessors Clive and Bob, Belinda seeks to be true to herself without external control. Cristoforou learns that she spends her days going to places where Sidley would hardly venture—hat shops, coffee bars, and cinemas showing horror movies. Despite Sidley's lectures on how to spend time efficiently, Belinda wanders about aimlessly. She admits to Sidley, "Most of my friends are all feelings. They're just like little moles bumping about in dark little burrows of feeling. And that was me too. Feeling, feeling all the time—but never getting to understand anything" (93). Belinda's liberal spirit conflicts with her husband's conservative nature. Belinda insists that she is not jealous when Sidley visits Madame Conchita's call girls or uses the Ladies Directory that he keeps hidden in his desk. She states, "Men should have a change from their wives occasionally" (110). On the other hand, Sidley hires a private investigator to shadow his wife even though she has been consistently faithful to him. Obviously, Sidley's imposing personality hinders the possibility of mutual trust and understanding between the accountant and his spouse.

Charles Sidley is determined to mold Belinda into the proper image of a wife of a successful professional man, even if it means restructuring his wife's personality. In his forties, Sidley is too young to be pompous, staid, and reserved. His "respect for fact" (64) and his "iceberg voice" (90) offer a facade by which he can evade reality. Belinda refers to his vocabulary as "All that morning suit language. It's only hiding" (90). Cristoforou also sees the staid accountant as artificial, fearful of life: "He's so afraid of being touched by life, he hardly exists. He's so scared of looking foolish, he puts up words against it for barriers: Good Taste, Morality. What you *should* do. What you *should* feel. He's walled up in Should like in a tomb" (110–111).

Sidley acknowledges that Belinda's personality was subsumed by the accountant's goal to remodel his wife in his own image: "Without my demanding it, of course, she surrendered her whole life to me, for remaking" (80). Recognizing that he had married an immature child without the cultural accoutrements necessary for social mobility, Sidley mistakenly tries to provide a sense of place for his wife in London society. Sidley proceeded to convert his spouse from waif to wife, much like Henry Higgins taking responsibility for Liza Doolittle's socialization. Sidley explains his awesome task to Cristoforou:

> Belinda is the wife of a professional man in a highly
> organized city in the twentieth century. That is her place.
> As I have often explained to her, this would undoubtedly

> be different if she were wedded to a jazz trumpeter in New
> Orleans, which she seems to think she is. There is no
> such thing as a perfectly independent person. (82)

Although he recognizes himself as a dilettante with regard to cultural literacy, Sidley upon first meeting Belinda plunged right into "the Theory of Natural Selection, the meaning of Id, Ego and Super-Ego, and . . . halfway through the structure of Bach's Fugue in C Sharp Minor, Book One, *Well-Tempered Clavier*" (93). Belinda acknowledges to Sidley that initially, "You gave me facts, ideas, reasons for things. You let me out of that hot, black burrow of feeling. I loved you then" (94). Her attitude changed, however, when Sidley insisted on molding her selection of hats and her taste in statuary, as well as providing advice with regard to how she should spend her leisure time and how to hold a saucepan properly at Cordon Bleu.

The disparity between Belinda's effervescent lifestyle and Sidley's reticence to experiment or to allow Belinda the opportunity to develop as an individual has created problems in their marriage. Dinners are spent in silence. Belinda's penchant for leather pajama suits makes her an unwelcome guest when her husband entertains his colleagues. Belinda complains of Sidley's patronizing attitude toward her: "You always say you want me to entertain your friends, and as soon as you can, you get out the port and send me out of the room" (90). Belinda wonders why Sidley, "surrounded by a lot of coughing old men with weak bladders and filthy tempers, scared of women and bright red with brandy" (90), could prefer the company of such friends to that of his young wife. Their relationship is not reciprocal because Sidley treats his wife like the pupil of "an awful headmaster," defending herself before the strict teacher (94). Thus, the spark in their marriage has become extinguished, as Belinda tries to explain to her husband:

> Love with me is a great burst of joy that someone exists.
> Just that. Breathes. And with that joy comes a huge great
> need to go out and greet them. Yes, that's the word:
> *greet*. I used to greet you, inside me anyway, forty times
> a day. Now it's once a fortnight. (95)

Belinda, feeling confined by Sidley's whims and wishes, says to him, "I feel I have to defend myself in front of you" (94), thereby virtually acknowledging the failure of their marriage: "It's all so dead with us now" (95).

Aware that the marriage is in a shambles, Belinda wanders throughout London to sort out the damage. When Cristoforou begins following her, instead of reacting in fear, she warms to the occasions because "all I knew was here was someone who approved of me" (98). Like Clive and Bob who were looking for positive encouragement rather than fatherly advice to develop their own sense of awareness, Belinda searches for a friend, not a mentor. Belinda explains to Sidley how Cristoforou differs from her husband: "What I was seeing was Approval. Simply that. Do you know, I'd forgotten what it was like to be looked at without criticism?" (97). Cristoforou admonishes Sidley, the headmaster, for upsetting the delicate balance in his marriage: "Your wife's affections weren't stolen, Mr. Sidley. They were going begging. ... (*Pause.*) And if you want them back, you must first learn how to get them" (103).

Julian Cristoforou is the catalyst who unites the seemingly incompatible spouses. He understands the importance of maintaining Belinda's individuality. As a free spirit, the private detective can empathize with Belinda's plight. Cristoforou, in his mid-thirties, *"breathes a gentle eccentricity, a nervousness combined with an air of almost meek self-disapprobation and a certain bright detachment"* (63). Inviting himself into Sidley's office without an appointment, Cristoforou eschews business decorum to adhere to his own personal whims. He calmly eats yoghurt, raisins, grapefruit, and macaroons in front of his employer, despite Sidley's obvious irritation with the private investigator's aplomb. He continually reminds Sidley of his individuality, noting, "I had twenty-three positions before I was thirty" (65) yet cautioning his employer about thinking that he is lackadaisical: "I never fail in jobs, they fail me" (65). Brandishing an obtrusive striped suit underneath his raincoat, and obviously shunning traditional office attire, Cristoforou proves himself to be anything but nondescript. He refuses to be labelled a conformist like Sidley's clients who "do what you tell them without question" (72). The importance of following his own set of values is indicated in the comical anecdote he tells of crashing his automobile into the baptismal font at Westminster Abbey in order to pursue an espionage suspect. Although Sidley is somewhat annoyed and impatient with the detective's eccentricity, Cristoforou is able to gain Sidley's attention because of his assertiveness and his commitment to his own high professional standards.

Cristoforou has spent three weeks following Belinda—and having her shadow him on alternate days. They pursued each other in silence, without ever speaking. Cristoforou states to her now, "I found you aimless in London; I gave you direction. I found you smileless; I gave you joy" (105). Even without benefit of formal discussion between them, Cristoforou fully understands the reason for the communication impasse between Belinda and her husband: "You're Spirit, Belinda, and he's Letter. You've got passion where all he's got is pronouncement" (111). Intimately aware of Belinda's need to express her individuality free from external control, Cristoforou devises a plan whereby Sidley must follow his wife every day for a month without speaking one word to her. Cristoforou believes that Belinda's meanderings will allow Sidley to explore new realms into which he has refrained from venturing. Joan F. Dean states that Cristoforou's scheme is Shaffer's way of affirming the viability of the family.[13] Dennis A. Klein believes the play's message to be that "imagination and fantasy are essentials in life (especially in marriage) and they keep everyday realities of life from becoming overbearing."[14] Nevertheless, Cristoforou's plan provides the significant insight into resolving the problem of the ill-fated marriage. By refusing to allow Sidley to talk to Belinda during their future sojourns in London, Cristoforou assures Belinda that the worldly advisor, who now must refrain from offering any advice, will not destroy the creativity and integrity of the individual. The detective thereby provides Belinda a chance to grow as an individual and to share that growth with someone she admires and once loved.

In each of these three early plays, Shaffer's message is to be true to yourself and trust your own instincts and values—despite any contrary advice imparted by others. In *Five Finger Exercise*, Clive is trying to find himself in an environment in which an authoritarian father and a doting mother impinge upon his emotional and intellectual growth. Bob's dilemma in *The Private Ear* is the result of relying on Ted's worldly knowledge instead of trusting his own unsophisticated judgment which would have been more harmonious with Doreen's parochialism. *The Public Eye* depicts the disastrous consequences that occur when one person's strict adherence to codified behavior completely subsumes and destroys the freedom of an individual with unconventional attitudes.

These early dramas provide a framework for the dialectic that we encounter in the later works between individual freedom and more carefully structured institutionalized behavior. Atahuallpa, Alan Strang, and Mozart inherit the problems of Clive Harrington, Bob, and Belinda—the chief significant difference being Shaffer's increasingly sophisticated skill at experimenting with stagecraft, structure, and rhythmic dialogue which turns his later plays into much more intricate artistry.

## Notes

1 . Peter Shaffer, "Preface," *The Collected Plays of Peter Shaffer* (New York: Harmony Books, 1982), p. viii.

2 . Joseph A. Loftus, "Playwright's Moral Exercise," *The New York Times*, 29 November 1959, Sec. 2, p. 1.

3 . Shaffer, "Preface," p. vii.

4 . Dennis A. Klein, *Peter Shaffer* (Boston: G. K. Hall, 1979), p. 33.

5 . Gore Vidal, "Strangers at Breakfast," *The Reporter*, 7 January 1960, p. 37.

6 . Joan F. Dean, "The Family as Microcosm in Shaffer's Plays," *Ball State University Forum*, 23, No. 1 (1982): 30.

7 . Peter Shaffer, *Five Finger Exercise* (New York: Harcourt, Brace and Company, 1958), p. 69. All subsequent citations are from this edition and are included within parentheses in the text.

8. At this point in the play, Clive feels that a vacation would be beneficial for both of them. Clive believes that Walter's dependence on the family is self-destructive; he therefore talks to Walter in good faith about a vacation. There is no evidence that Clive is making a homosexual gesture here or that Walter interprets the invitation in a sexual manner. For an opposing viewpoint that stresses a possible sexual relationship between Clive and Walter—which some critics think Louise also senses—see Charles A. Pennel, "The Plays of Peter Shaffer: Experiment in Convention," *Kansas Quarterly*, 3, No. 2 (1971): 102, and Oleg Kerensky, *The New British Drama: Fourteen Playwrights Since Osborne and Pinter* (London: Hamish Hamilton, 1977), p. 33.

9. See Barry Pree, "Peter Shaffer," *The Transatlantic Review*, 14 (Autumn 1963): 63, and Shaffer. "Preface," p. ix.

10. Peter Shaffer, *The Private Ear and The Public Eye* (New York: Stein and Day, 1964), p. 31. All subsequent citations are from this edition and are included within parentheses in the text.

11. Pennel, "The Plays of Peter Shaffer: Experiment in Convention," p. 103.

12. For a comparison between Peter Grimes and Bob, see Klein, *Peter Shaffer*, 61, and Rodney Simard, *Postmodern Drama: Contemporary Playwrights in America and Britain* (Lanham, Md.: University Press of America, Inc., 1984), p. 106.

13. Dean, "The Family as Microcosm in Shaffer's Plays," p. 32.

14. Klein, *Peter Shaffer*, p. 68.

# THE COSMIC EMBRACE: PETER SHAFFER'S METAPHYSICS

## Barbara Lounsberry

Any discussion of metaphysics in the plays of Peter Shaffer must begin with a definition of terms. Historically, the word "metaphysics" was first applied to the thirteen books of Aristotle which dealt with questions of "first philosophy" or being. Metaphysics came to refer to that branch of speculative inquiry which treats of the first principles of things, including such concepts as being, substance, essence, time, space, cause, and identity. Metaphysicians traditionally have interpreted the natural world and theorized on the existence and nature of God.

In the twentieth century, however, metaphysics has fallen on hard times. Ludwig Wittgenstein and the Logical Positivists have argued that metaphysical assertions are meaningless because they seek to describe a region that exists outside the realm that language can illuminate. As a result, many twentieth-century philosophers have been reluctant to try to construct *a priori* proofs of the existence of God or of the immortality of the soul. As Gilbert Ryle defines "Metaphysics" in our time, "*A priori* cosmology and *a priori* theology are both suspect, and the term 'metaphysics' is widely, though not universally treated either as a redundant synonym of 'philosophy' or else as a valedictory label for those suspect enterprises" (*Encyclopedia Britannica*, 1973 ed.).

In such a devalued climate, Peter Shaffer's explorations of the nature of being and the existence and nature of God seem particularly heroic. His work in "total theater" may be seen as an answer to the Logical Positivists, for he goes beyond language to the power of music, mime, masks, rites, chants, bird calls, hoofbeats, and vivid visual spectacle to evoke and explore metaphysical themes. It should be said at the outset that Shaffer is not a systematic metaphysician. Unlike Sartre, he does not dramatize a particular metaphysical school of thought. Nevertheless, as many readers and critics have noted, Shaffer has shown himself to be vitally interested in "first questions" of being, identity, freedom, and what he has called the "sense of the divine."[1] By describing how Shaffer's works interact with such philosophical studies as logic, epistemology, ethics, and aesthetics, I will seek to define Shaffer's evolving metaphysical position.

## Logic and Lies: *Lettice and Lovage*

I mention logic only to dismiss it. Shaffer does as much throughout his nine works in *The Collected Plays*,[2] as well as in his latest comedy, *Lettice and Lovage*.[3] In plays such as *The Public Eye* and *Lettice and Lovage*, accountants and lawyers (society's embodiments of logic and rational argument) are co-opted by characters representing less orderly but more imaginative visions. In *The Public Eye*, chartered accountant Charles Sidley is "Letter" while his wife Belinda is "Spirit" (142); what is needed and effected by Shaffer is a synthesis of the two. Charles' logic, Belinda testifies, originally offered her liberation. "You gave me facts, ideas, reasons for things. You let me out of that hot, black burrow of feeling. I loved you then" (131), she tells her husband. Charles, however, has been unable to reciprocate by absorbing Belinda's Spirit. "He's so scared of looking foolish," Cristoforou says of Sidley, "he puts up words against [life] for barriers" (142). At play's end, the man of logic is deprived of ledgers and language. According to Cristoforou's regimen, Sidley will learn by following the witch, Belinda.

Facts and solicitors are similarly "Enlarged . . . Enlivened . . . and Enlightened" in *Lettice and Lovage*. Here, solicitor Bardolph is caught up in the Falstaffian revels. "Transported," he "moves uninhibitedly around the room at a slow and menacing march, banging his invisible drum and calling out his 'pam-tititi-pams' with increasing excitement" (85). More centrally, Lotte—gatekeeper of factual accuracy at the Preservation Trust—learns that facts can be "mere" and in need of someone to "take a hand" (23). She learns the meaning of *lovage* which is herbal as well as verbal (44, 48).

Shaffer administers the definitive defeat to reason, however, in his only unproduced drama, *Shrivings*. In this play, the eminent philosopher Gideon Petrie is unmasked and his rationalism discredited. Poet Mark Askelon calls Gideon a "thoroughgoing rationalist" (328) and the "First Pope of Reason" (331). Shrivings he labels the "Cathedral of Humanism" (331). When tested, however, Gideon's rational pacifism proves false. In Act II, when Mark is tied to the "throne of reason" (331), he first is tortured then destroyed by the disciples of non-violence. In the final act, Gideon himself raises his hand in violence.

Shaffer presents Gideon's rational pacifism as the philosophy of an adolescent idealist, of one who does not perceive clearly. "Saint Gideon Petrie on his peacock throne of Reason, ringed by the irises of adolescence!" Mark taunts (347). Lois Neal, the young American who figuratively "kneels" in worship of Gideon's rational humanism, is herself unmasked and brought painfully to adult understanding in the course of the conflict. Speaking of Gideon's principled pacifism, Mark tells her, "It's a lovely vision, Miss Neal. Many of us dreamed it once. And then woke" (357). Lois herself comes to acknowledge that Gideon's eyes are gummy and "disgusting" (375). "They're never really *on you*," she says, to which *Ask*elon queries, "As if they're . . . out of focus?" (375).

Askelon forces master and disciples to acknowledge that violence is an unalterable facet of human nature, indeed of nature itself. "Acolytes of the unalterable: unite!" he cries. "Let's wear our green with courage! Green for nature! For the returning cycles of our agony!" (359). Recognition of the violence inherent in "God's hand" leaves Gideon and Lois in the state of adult despair. Gideon walks up and down the room "caged in pain" (388). At the play's conclusion, both stare rigidly before them, and only Gideon finally bows his head to a murderer's hand.

## Epistemology

Peter Shaffer thus has little interest in logic or pure rationality; his metaphysics are those of a mystic attuned to the supra-rational mysteries of existence. Just as he pursues no systematic theory of logic, Shaffer offers no thoroughgoing epistemology or theory of knowledge. Nevertheless, it is possible to construct his epistemological position from the plays themselves. In the ongoing debate between empiricists and rationalists, and between the Correspondence Theory of Truth and the Coherence Theory of Truth, Shaffer assuredly would decline taking sides. He would probably seek a synthesis of the positions, arguing that the claims of both rationality and observation must be honored. As a writer he is compelled to dramatize his metaphysical quests in concrete, empirical terms. Gods in Shaffer's plays come in the form of suns, horses, and music. They are empirical, rational, and more.

Shaffer is far, however, from a materialist. In each of his plays, from *Five Finger Exercise* to *Lettice and Lovage*, spiritual issues take precedence over material concerns which are seen as detracting from proper spirituality. Material success means little to Clive in *Five Finger Exercise*, Bob in *The Private Ear*, or Belinda in *The Public Eye*. It means nothing to Pizarro in *The Royal Hunt of the Sun*, Alan and Dysart in *Equus*, Mark Askelon in *Shrivings*, Salieri in *Amadeus*, and Lettice and Lotte in *Lettice and Lovage*. All are seeking spiritual rather than material fulfillment.[4] In *The Royal Hunt of the Sun* and *Equus*, economic materialism is particularly decried. The Spaniards in their greed destroy the Incan civilization. They literally tear the gold from the sun. They are "robber finches" who steal gold and destroy souls. In *Equus*, Alan Strang's "foes" are the "Hosts of Hoover. The Hosts of Philco. The Hosts of Pufco. The House of Remington and all its tribe" (447).

Thus Shaffer finds little to be derived from materialism per se, and still less from social institutions. All human institutions— including those of the family, state, army, and church—are false idols which ultimately corrupt and destroy purer forms of being, knowledge, and worship in Shaffer's plays.[5] The "five finger exercise" implied in the title of Shaffer's first produced play depicts a family which nearly

strangles Clive and Walter, just as it warps Alan Strang in *Equus*. The
Catholic Church bestows its blessings on the destruction of the Incas,
just as Christian fundamentalism has blood on its hand in *Equus*. In
*Shrivings*, Shaffer succinctly offers his indictment of institutionalism
in all its forms in parallel speeches by Gideon and Mark:

> GIDEON:     You've been given expert courses in all the
>            right subjects. Mangerism, or worship of
>            Family; Flaggism, or worship of Tribe;
>            Thingism, or worship of Money. In our
>            theaters and on our screens we have taught
>            you to find the act of killing men exciting,
>            and the act of creating them obscene. You
>            can go to church, and respect the stopped
>            mind. You can go to war memorials, and
>            respect the stopped body. (340)
>
>            . . . . .
>
> MARK:       Isn't it amusing how the fashions in
>            Inquisition stay the same? . . . First we have
>            the vengeful Daddy, wrapped in clouds. Then
>            Mobile Mary, whizzing up in Heaven. Now
>            it's Self-Raising Man, jumping himself out
>            of nature: what an astonishing sight! (359)

If Shaffer has little interest in materialism and scorn for
institutions, what then is he *for*? He is true to the teachings of the
Logical Positivists in asserting that human beings can have no certain
knowledge of God or of the meaning of existence. The settings of many
of Shaffer's plays are emblems of the human condition as he sees it: a
bare stage and an upper level. This setting of *The Royal Hunt of the
Sun*, suggesting a stark existence below and a higher (Godly) state
above, is recreated in different guises in *Shrivings* and *Amadeus*.
Destruction occurs on both levels in Shaffer's plays, in the earthly
realm and above.[6]

Placed on these bi-level sets, Shaffer's characters usually are
stripped bare, physically and psychically, in the course of the drama.
The primal nudity of Alan and Jill in *Equus* immediately comes to
mind, but we forget that David and Lois are naked under white towels in
the final act of *Shrivings*, and that a recurring Shaffer motif is a youth

shivering under blankets. These blankets seem to represent
psychological covers and institutional wrappings which Shaffer will
remove to reveal human beings in their naked, shivering, and vulnerable
natural state.[7]

Stripped of social and psychological shields, Shaffer's characters
exist in pain and torment. *The Royal Hunt of the Sun* even places its
*audience* as well as the Spaniards in Plato's cave, trying to separate
shadow from substance: "The lights snap out and, lit from the side, the
rays of the metal sun throw long shadows across the wooden wall"
(266). Pizarro says to Atahuallpa, "Trapped in this cage we cry out,
'There's a jailer; there must be. At the last, last, last of lasts he will let
us out. He will! He will!' . . . But, oh, my boy, no one will come for
all our crying" (298). The psychiatrist Martin Dysart in *Equus* says, "I
need . . . a way of seeing in the dark. What way is this? . . . *What dark
is this*?" and he comes closer even than Pizarro to acceptance of cosmic
ignorance. "All right—I say it!" he states at play's end: "In an ultimate
sense I cannot know what I do in this place" (476). Indeed, in *Equus*
Shaffer comes closest to embracing phenomenology, only to end by
reaffirming humanity's faulty knowledge:

> A child is born into a world of phenomena all equal in
> their power to enslave. . . . Suddenly one strikes. Why?
> Moments snap together like magnets, forging a chain of
> shackles. Why? I can trace them. I can even, with time,
> pull them apart again. But why at the start they were ever
> magnetized at all—just those particular moments of
> experience and no others—I don't know. *And nor does
> anyone else.* (450)

"Beloved God, this silence!" the fortune teller Sophie exclaims in
*The White Liars.* "You'd think *someone* would consult me, if only to
ask should they kill themselves" (154). Even in Shaffer's comedies, the
torment of not-knowing is present. At first viewing, few would suspect
Shaffer's ingenious farce *Black Comedy* has anything to do with
metaphysics. Yet the entire conception can be seen as an emblem of the
human predicament. Schuppanzigh, the German electrician whose name
sounds like "chimpanzee," becomes a mocking figure of God in the
comedy. "Here's now an end to your troubles!" he says:

> Like Jehovah in the sacred Testament, I give you the
> most miraculous gift of the Creation! Light! . . . Attend
> all of you. God said: "Let there be light!" And there was,
> good  people,  suddenly!—astoundingly!
> instantaneously—inconceivably—inexhaustibly—
> inextinguishably and eternally—LIGHT!
> [SCHUPPANZIGH, *with a great flourish, flicks the light
> switch. Instant darkness.*] (238)

In an ultimate dark jest, what God calls light is darkness to us.
Brindsley's "feeling ahead of him, trying to part the darkness with his
hands" (190) becomes a mime of the human condition.

According to Shaffer's metaphysics, we do not and cannot know
with any certainty the meaning of life (if there is one) or whether God
exists. Despite this harsh reality, we nevertheless seek meaning and
worship. Shaffer's ouevre can be seen as an exploration of this poignant
paradox. As he confessed in 1980, "I just feel in myself that there is a
constant debate going on between . . . the secular side of me [and] the
fact that I have never actually been able to buy anything of official
religion—and the inescapable fact that to me a life without a sense of
the divine is perfectly meaningless."[8] From *Royal Hunt* on, we can
watch Shaffer seek the divine, first in nature, then in art, and finally in
the abstract and ineffable cosmic embrace of love.

In *Royal Hunt* Shaffer seeks god in nature, in the daily renewing
miracle of the sun. Pizarro says to DeSoto, "I myself can't fix anything
nearer to a thought of worship than standing at dawn and watching [the
sun] fill the world. Like the coming of something eternal against going
flesh" (272). Later, he explains to Young Martin, "What else is god but
what we know we can't do without? The flowers that worship [the sun],
the sunflowers in their soil, are us after night, after cold and lightless
days, turning our faces to [the sun] adoring" (307). That the sun's rays
do not revive the "son of the sun," Atahuallpa, is seen by many as
Shaffer's ultimate rejection of the sun as deity, but as I have argued
elsewhere, Atahuallpa's resurrection scene is highly ambiguous.
Although Atahuallpa himself does not rise, a miracle of sorts does
occur. The sunlight brightens on *Pizarro's* head as he sheds the first tear
of his life. The meeting of Pizarro and Atahuallpa has brought them
both a greater love than either has heretofore experienced. In this

respect, Atahuallpa's sacrifice has saved one soul, and passed the godhead onto him. Pizarro carries his joy for a few minutes only before sinking back into despair, but the moment testifies not only to the nobility of his and Atahuallpa's enterprise, but to his later statement that there must be "some immortal business surely" in "making whatever God there is" (310).

The Incan legend is that "Here on earth Gods come one after another" (285), and this is central to Shaffer's sense of worship. In *Equus*, the play that followed *Royal Hunt*, Shaffer continues seeking God in nature, but now in a multiplicity of nature spirits. Here the Sun God is replaced by the related Greek image of the horse as God, and Alan Strang, who has created and worships Equus, insists that his God lives in all horses (441). Martin Dysart, Alan's psychiatrist, exclaims to the magistrate Hesther Salomon:

> Look! Life is only comprehensible through a thousand local Gods. And not just the old dead ones with names like Zeus—no, but living Geniuses of Place and Person! And not just Greece but modern England! Spirits of certain trees, certain curves of brick wall, certain chip shops, if you like, and slate-roofs—just as of certain frowns in people and slouches. . . . Worship as many as you can see—and more will appear! (438)

Here Shaffer seems to champion animism and a transcendental belief in God in all things.[9] "Without worship you shrink, it's as brutal as that," Dysart declares. *Equus* should be viewed as yet another Shaffer challenge, not only to Martin Dysart, but to the audience, to break the reins of "old language and old assumptions" and leap "clean-hoofed on to a whole new track of being [we] only suspect is there" (*Equus* 402). In *Royal Hunt*, Pizarro had articulated a similar desire in his visions of the New World. "[S]omething in me was longing for a new place," he tells DeSoto, "like a country after rain, washed clear of all the badges and barriers, the pebbles men drop to tell them where they are" (271). To Shaffer, such new worlds, or new tracks of being, can only be found through worship of unknowable gods.

## Ethics

Given only the certainty of uncertainty about the existence of God and the meaning of life, ethics in Shaffer's plays are necessarily spare and tentative. They exist nevertheless. Shaffer appears to be more interested in normative ethics than in meta-ethics. The simple ethical positions advanced in his plays appear to be objective rather than subjective; they are declarations of ethical truths divorced from subjective points of view. Furthermore, Shaffer can be classified as an ethical *intuitionist* rather than an ethical *naturalist*. Ethical positions advanced in his plays rest on no empirical verification; they are simply intuited and declared.

Shaffer's sense of the "good" and the "right" might seem as a retort to Socrates' position that it is always better to suffer than to do evil. The dramatist's works demonstrate that human beings must suffer *and* do evil; choice appears impossible. Even the best of Shaffer's characters end up harming others.

The ethical tenets articulated in Shaffer's plays most closely reflect the Moral Sense theory of ethics proposed by the Earl of Shaftsbury and his disciple Francis Hutcheson in the seventeenth and eighteenth centuries. Shaftsbury asserted that human beings possess a natural sympathy leading to benevolence, social interest, and commitment to the public good. For Shaftsbury, the sensing of virtue in actions is comparable to the sensing of beauty in art; thus the test of a proposed action is whether it contributes to the general harmony of mankind.

Only four characters in Shaffer's plays speak with any degree of admirable ethical authority. They are Atahuallpa, DeSoto, and Young Martin in *Royal Hunt*, and Hesther Salomon in *Equus*. The playwright's remaining characters are either moral hypocrites or searchers. Atahuallpa, DeSoto, and Young Martin all speak for "trust" and for the integrity of one's word. Atahuallpa trusts Pizarro to keep his promise. DeSoto insists that Pizarro meet this ethical standard: "He [Atahuallpa] trusts you, trust him," DeSoto urges. "It's all you can do. . . . I wish to God you'd never made this bargain. But you did. Now you've no choice left" (302). Pizarro reveals his tragic hubris when he replies, "In Peru I am absolute. I have choice always," to which DeSoto replies, "I'm not playing words, General. There's no choice where you don't stick by it" (302). Young Martin earlier advocates the same moral stance:

> YOUNG MARTIN:   He trusts you, sir.
> PIZARRO:             Trust: what's that? Another word! Honor
>                              . . . glory . . . trust: your word-Gods!
>
>                              . . . . .
>
> YOUNG MARTIN [*greatly daring*]: You can't betray him,
>                              sir. You can't (296–297)

But Pizarro can. The prevalence of lying and betrayal in Shaffer's plays testifies to the importance he places on "honesty" and "trust," and to the rarity of these virtues in human society as he sees it. Though Pizarro has sought to dismiss "trust" and "honor" as "word-Gods," at the end of the play he comes to a deeper understanding of their importance:

> The sky has no feelings, but we know them, that's sure.
> Martin's hope, and DeSoto's honor, and your trust—your
> trust which hunted me: we alone make these. That's some
> marvel, yes, some marvel. To sit in a great cold silence,
> and sing out sweet with just our own warm breath: that's
> some marvel, surely. (310)

"Trust" rests on human sympathy and is a social virtue. Hesther Salomon (her name suggesting the wisdom of Solomon) even more firmly represents these ethics as the compassionate magistrate of *Equus*. She functions as the ethical spur whenever Dysart doubts the wisdom of treating Alan. "I suppose one of the few things one can do is simply hold on to priorities," she tells Dysart early in the drama. "Like what?" he inquires. "Oh—children before grownups. Things like that" (439). This is the kind of spare morality which Shaffer can endorse. Later, Hesther will base her counsel on her sympathy and sense of social harmony. "The boy's in pain, Martin. That's all I see. In the end," she insists (455). "Worship isn't destructive, Martin. I know that" (453), she adds.

Honesty, trust, honor. Children before grownups. Administering to pain and seeking to lighten the inevitable destruction. These are simple "goods," but they represent an ethical system on which to build a civilization.

## Aesthetics

Shaffer's theory of the beautiful in art and nature can also be traced to the Moral Sense teachings of Shaftsbury and Hutcheson who interpreted beauty in terms of a special inner "sense" responsive to harmony. Bob has this inner sense in the well-named *Private Ear*, as do Mark and David in *Shrivings*, Mozart and Salieri in *Amadeus*, and Lotte in *Lettice and Lovage*. Shaffer's aesthetics also borrow from Aristotle and Plotinus, Thomas Aquinas, Hegel, and Jacques Maritain. The worshipers of artistic beauty in Shaffer's plays (and, indeed, the plays themselves) endorse Aristotle's dictum that beauty depends on organic unity, a unity in which every part contributes to the quality of the whole. This tenet is revealed in the very title *Five Finger Exercise*, as well as in a moving statement by Mozart in *Amadeus:*

> I tell you I want to write a finale lasting half an hour! A quartet becoming a quintet becoming a sextet. On and on, wider and wider—all sounds multiplying and rising together—and then together making a sound entirely new! . . . I bet you that's how God hears the world. Millions of sounds ascending at once and mixing in His ear to become an unending music, unimaginable to us! [*To Salieri.*] That's our job! That's our job, we composers: to combine the inner minds of him and him and him, and her and her—the thoughts of chambermaids and Court Composers—and turn the audience into God. (527)

Shaffer's works also reflect the aesthetic teachings of his fellow neoclassical mystic Plotinus, who associated the beautiful with a radiance or splendor resulting from the quality of unity. Such radiance can be seen in Bob's print of Botticelli's "Birth of Venus" in *The Private Ear*, as well as in the love duet from *Madame Butterfly* which he plays on the record player. Radiance and splendor surround Atahuallpa in *Royal Hunt* and exude from Mozart's music in *Amadeus*, particularly in the scene from *The Magic Flute*. For Plotinus and for Shaffer such radiance is a divine principle which is more or less completely reflected in the world.

Thomas Aquinas added to this notion the insistence that beauty is related to the cognitive function. For Aquinas, beautiful objects must have proportion or harmony, brightness or clarity, and integrity or perfection. This tradition has been carried forward in the twentieth century by Jacques Maritain who considered art as a concrete embodiment of beauty which he defined as both pleasing to the intellect and a sign of something more divine. With Hegel, Shaffer shares the sense of beauty as the Absolute shining through appearance and a sense of the importance of passion in the creation of Absolute Beauty.

Bob in *The Private Ear* is Shaffer's first true disciple of the beautiful. Bob speaks passionately of the "spiritual beauty" of Botticelli's "Birth of Venus." "That's what that picture really represents," Bob tells Ted. "The birth of beauty in the human soul" (84). Quoting from his art book, Bob declares that "Venus is the Mother of Grace, of Beauty, and of Faith" (84). Bob's torment lies in the fact that the spiritual beauty he perceives is unrecognized by his contemporaries.

Mark and David Askelon in *Shrivings* are both artists of the beautiful. David makes beautiful furniture, while his father crafts volumes of poems. One wishes Shaffer would bring even more clarity to this aesthetic dimension of *Shrivings*. Mark Askelon's true worship seems to be of poetry. "Even atheism itself ran out, the moment I felt one poem as an act of worship," Mark states (376). The battle of Shrivings, then, is not between "humanism" and "atheism," but between Reason and Art. Mark, however, appears to be a blocked artist. Speaking to Lois of her eyes (a traditional symbol of divinity), Mark confesses: "If I could once make them in a poem, I'd never open my mouth again" (378). But apparently he cannot. Shaffer never makes it clear if we are to consider Mark's early volumes of "revolutionary" poetry beautiful and authentic. He fails to indicate the precise moment Mark ceased to live in the "now" and became spiritually "dead." Readers of *Shrivings* are left with important questions. As a blocked poet, is

Mark Askelon a legitimate champion of Art? Would a more interesting target for his destruction be the authentic artist, his son?

This, of course, becomes (with slight variations) the plot of *Amadeus*, Shaffer's most direct engagement of metaphysical questions to date. With *Amadeus* the dramatist moves from locating God in nature to exploring at great length the possibility of divinity in art. "Music is God's art," Salieri affirms (488). "It is only through hearing, music that I know God exists" (557). Music partakes of the absolute. "A note of music is either right or wrong—*absolutely*!" Salieri insists. "Not even Time can alter that" (488). In *Amadeus* Shaffer introduces two new ideas regarding the divine: divine need and divine use. "God needed Mozart to let himself into the world," Salieri declares (521). When he first hears Mozart's music, Salieri senses that the pain it causes him is the pain of God's "need":

> The squeezebox groaned louder, and over it the higher
> instruments wailed and warbled, throwing lines of sound
> around me—long lines of pain around and through me—
> ah, the pain! Pain as I had never known it. . . . [*Calling
> up in agony.*] "*What?! What is this? Tell me, Signore!*
> What is this *pain* ? What is this *need* in the sound?
> Forever unfulfillable yet fulfilling him who hears it,
> utterly! Is it *Your* need? . . . *Can it be Yours?* (497)

This is Shaffer's first suggestion that Gods have needs, just as humans do. Salieri also seems to suggest that while God can fulfill human needs, His needs remain forever unfulfilled.

Intriguingly, though the God depicted by Salieri may feel pain and need, this God (in his view) lacks other emotions, such as pity and love. As a result, God (to Salieri) is simply an exploiter. "God does not love you, Amadeus!" Salieri cries, underscoring the irony of Mozart's name: "God does not love! He can only *use*! . . . He cares nothing for who He uses; nothing for who He denies!" (552). In this vision of divinity, God is an insensitive user: "God blew—as He must—without cease," Salieri reports. "The flute split in the mouth of his insatiable need" (555).

Thus Shaffer makes his own addition to aesthetic theory: the assertion that the beautiful is always destroyed. Stretching out his hand in a "vicious gesture," Bob scratches the Puccini record in *The Private Ear,* deliberately "damaging it beyond repair" (107). Human hands drop the lovely statue of Buddha in *Black Comedy,* and, by all accounts, it is the truest work of beauty in Brindsley's apartment. The Spaniards loot the sun and destroy the priceless Incan art objects, just as God's vessel, Mozart, is destroyed in *Amadeus.*

Beauty and destruction are thus inseparable in Shaffer, just as are worship and destruction. In Shaffer's metaphysics and aesthetics, both creation and destruction are part of God's "hand." Humanity, created in the image of the Great Creator/Destroyer, simply reflects His nature.

## The Cosmic Embrace

Despite this perilous condition, throughout his ten published dramas, and particularly in his four most recent plays, Peter Shaffer has explored the possibility of love and reconciliation between an unknowable and destructive God and his destructive and despairing creations. Shaffer's characters clearly long for such love and reconciliation. Throughout his plays, Shaffer expresses this yearning in the recurring image of hands and arms extending outward in a gesture of embrace. This poignant Shafferian mime of cosmic yearning has three characteristics: (1) a character reaches out hands and arms, seeking the embrace of love; (2) the other "loved one" is usually depicted as "foreign," indicating the estrangement between humanity and its loved objects or "Gods"; and (3) the other frequently will refuse the embrace.

In *Five Finger Exercise* both Walter and Clive seek the loving acceptance of Louise Harrington. In Act I, Louise takes Walter's head in her hands and holds it close to her (31). This embrace is filial for Walter, sexual for Louise. In Act II, when Louise hears Walter play the "warm slow movement" of the Brahms Symphony, she draws a surrogate, Clive, to her. "He allows himself to be drawn," Shaffer's stage directions note, and "a brief instant of great intimacy recurs, as it happened in the first scene" (47). Here, the filial and sexual are intermingled for both partners in a complex way. Clive, we should realize, equates personal growth with love and worship. "I want to fall in love with just one person," he tells Walter. "To know what it is to bless and be blessed. And to serve a great cause with devotion" (65).

Clive indeed has made a foreign figurehead of his mother. He calls her his Empress and treats her with obeisance. But at play's end, when he "kneels to [his 'Empress'] and embraces her with desperate tenderness" in a moment designed to "echo the two preceding ones," Louise "shakes him off" (72). The embrace of love is denied.

Bob's embrace of Behemoth, his stereo phonograph, at the end of *The Private Ear* is a variation on this embrace. Both Behemoth and Louise are "monsters" tendering unrealizable love. Bob "kneels to [Behemoth], stretching out his arms to enfold it" (106). This embrace, like Clive's, however, only leads to destruction. In *The White Liars* Frank also has first made a "monster" of Tom, and then embraced his exotic lower-class "creation." The unmasked Tom reaches out his hand to Frank in a more honest gesture of reconciliation before he leaves, but the gesture is not met (177).

Reconciliation is also uncertain in *The Public Eye*, a comedy in which Shaffer's cosmic embrace is described rather than enacted, intimating that it can be a spiritual as well as physical gesture. Speaking to Charles, Belinda says:

> Love with me is a great burst of joy that someone exists. Just that. Breathes! And with that joy comes a huge great need to go out and greet them. Yes, that's the word: *greet*. I used to greet you, inside me anyway, forty times a day. Now it's once a fortnight. (132)

*The Public Eye* ends, however, with only the hope that this greeting will increase—and be reciprocated.

In *Black Comedy* Shaffer introduces the "Hand Game" during which grasping and recognizing hands become signs of spiritual affinity. Ultimately Brindsley embraces the more exotic Clea (short, perhaps, for Cleopatra) rather than the conventional Carol; however, in the repetition of cosmic destruction, Clea bites Brindsley's hand and he falls to his knees in "silent agony" (228). In *The Royal Hunt of the Sun*, Pizarro reaches out his hand to Atahuallpa only finally to slap the worshiper who sought him as God.

From *Equus* and *Shrivings* on, however, the playwright has ventured moments of greater love and reconciliation. Alan Strang, like the majority of Shaffer's characters, has a profound need for the embrace of love. (Alan appears to have found it in moments of unity with his god Nugget. In a mime of the human condition, Alan undresses completely before the animal. "When he is finished, and obviously quite naked," state the stage directions, "he throws out his arms and shows himself fully to his God, bowing his head before Nugget" (445). Nugget reciprocates by bowing his head into Alan's palm (445). Indeed in the play's opening tableau (repeated in Dysart's later description), Alan's "head is pressed against the shoulder of the horse, his hands stretching up to fondle its head. The horse in turn nuzzles his neck" (401). This moment of reciprocal embrace in *Equus*, as in Shaffer's earlier plays, cannot, however, be sustained. Here the human hand of love becomes the hand of destruction. Yet Alan's great need—he clings to a nurse, to Dysart, and even momentarily embraces Jill—underscores the importance of the embrace of love.

Nugget's bowing his head to eat from Alan's hand is echoed at the close of Shaffer's next play, *Shrivings*, when Gideon bows his head to eat from murderer Mark Askelon's extended hand. However, earlier in the play a richer moment of cosmic embrace occurs between David Askelon, the genuine artist, and his despairing father, Mark. Significantly, here the urge to destruction is checked and the cosmic embrace achieved, as indicated by Shaffer's crucial stage directions:

> *[David's] hands fly up, join violently above his head.*
> *For a long moment they stay up there, poised to smash*
> *his father down. Then he begins to tremble. Slowly his*
> *arms are lowered over his father's head. He pulls Mark to*
> *him, and kisses him on the face. They stay still. (392)*

David then shuts the door of the shrine of the false foreign Goddess Guilia, and instructs his father to reach out to Gideon in love.

Mozart in *Amadeus* is even more capable than David or Alan of the cosmic embrace. At the age of six, he jumps into Marie Antoinette's arms, kisses her on both cheeks, and asks, "Will you marry me: yes or no?" (500). His later kissing of hands at the Hapsburg court is labeled too "extravagant," however, by the conventional Emperor and his sycophants, yet even at the end of a hard life Mozart has not lost his ability to leap into embrace. In one of the most heartbreaking moments in the play, Mozart "extends his arms upward, imploringly to Salieri" and deliriously cries:

> Take me, Papa. Take me. Put down your arms and I'll hop into them. Just as we used to do it. . . . Hop-hop-hop-hop-UP! [*He jumps up on the table, and embraces Salieri, who stands horrified and unmoving.*] Hold me close to you, Papa. Let's sing our little Kissing Song together. (552–553)

Salieri, though, "disengages himself" (553). Fortunately the well-named Constanze appears on the scene, and Mozart "virtually falls off the table into her arms" (553). Mozart's physical embrace is echoed in his music, where in his *Magic Flute* he takes the ironic sign of Masonic "brotherly love," the closed fist, and transforms it into "a priestly figure extending its arms to the world in universal greeting" (548). Mozart's artistic journey appears to be that of David Askelon in *Shrivings*: "No more an accusing figure, but forgiving! The Highest Priest of the Order—his hand extended to the world in love!" (548).[10]

In his most recent drama, the comedy *Lettice and Lovage*, Shaffer also dramatizes reconciliation which resists institutional destruction. In Act I, Lettice's consecutive versions of the Fustian family history should be seen as increasingly more vivid parables of cosmic embrace. In the comparatively tame first version, Queen Elizabeth I would have fallen "had not her host taken hold of her arm and saved her" (4). Even in this version, the Queen reciprocates Fustian's gesture by dubbing him a knight, thus elevating his position. In Lettice's third version, however, John Fustian demonstrates Mozartian heights. While the hundred other guests stand frozen, "arms outstretched in powerless gesture," Fustian moves. "He who up to that moment has lived his whole life as a dull and turgid yeoman," Lettice stresses, "breaks the spell! Springs forward—upward—rises like a bird—like feathered Mercury—*soars* in one astounding leap the whole height of these stairs, and at the last possible moment catches her in his loyal arms, raises her high above his head, and rose-cheeked with triumph cries up to her: 'Adored Majesty! Adored and Endored Majesty!'" (8). In her recounting of Lettice's lecture, Lotte reiterates the scene of cosmic love presented earlier in both *Equus* and *Shrivings*: "[John Fustian's] actually feeding fried hedgehogs into Queen Elizabeth's mouth directly from his fingers" (15).

Lettice admits that sometimes she "takes a hand" to life (22–23). Lotte, we discover, is in sore need of this hand. She is one of Shaffer's disciples of the beautiful who has lost her way. "I am not a Christian," she tells Lettice, "and the only good I perceive is in beauty" (46). Lotte's vision and being have been stifled, however, not only by twentieth-century English architecture, but by her very occupation as head of the Preservation Trust. The spirit she requires rests in Lettice Douffet, a professed "foreigner" with whom she, like Shaffer's other worshipers, seeks alliance. "I imagine I appear rather an alien person to you," Lettice says to Lotte, who replies, "That is not all bad, I suspect" (44).

Lettice's basement apartment, with the tantalizing half-level of street visible above, parallels the subterranean setting of *The White Liars* where growth can occur. In this sub-conscious world, Lettice and Lotte enact the creative and destructive sides of the cosmic embrace. In a moment of physical and spiritual unmasking in Act II, Lotte kneels before Lettice and asks for her hand: "Tentatively Lettice extends her hand to Lotte's head. . . . Lettice touches Lotte's hair and then pulls it. It comes away in her hand: it is a wig. Beneath it is revealed a head of fluffy grey hair" (58). Lettice's reaction is more than mere acceptance: "Oh wonderful, wonderful! *Wonderful—beyond measure*! [A pause] Please—have dinner just like that" (58)

In Act III, we learn that the reclaimed worshiper has been attacked, first by the claws of Lettice's "familiar" (the cat Felina, Queen of Sorrows), and then by the axe from Lettice's hand. Once again the dramatist insists that destruction is part of the divine embrace. Yet true reconciliation occurs at the end of *Lettice and Lovage*, for Lettice hands flowers into Lotte's arms—a gesture of love and reconciliation. "You are—indispensable" Lotte affirms of the daring and unpredictable Lettice. "My life began again when I first walked down those stairs [of Lettice's flat]" (94).

Like Shakespeare's *The Tempest* or *A Winter's Tale*, *Lettice and Lovage* can be seen as a fantastical parable of Shaffer's dramatic enterprises. He seeks to make us creative (and creators) in his dramas. Through his imaginative vision, he seeks to "Enlargen, Enliven, and

Enlighten" us; indeed, he recognizes the need to turn the cannon on us to destroy the ugly narrowness of our worlds and bombard us into greater being. Never masking the danger and uncertainty of this enterprise, he allows us the evocative visions of *his* cosmic embrace.

# Notes

1. Brian Connell, "Peter Shaffer: The Two Sides of Theatre's Agonised Perfectionist," *The Times [London]*, 28 April 1980, p. 7.

2. Peter Shaffer, *The Collected Plays of Peter Shaffer* (New York: Harmony Books, 1982). Citations to Shaffer's plays—except for *Lettice and Lovage* —will come from this edition, with page references in my essay noted in parentheses.

3. *Lettice and Lovage[:] A Comedy in Three Acts* (London: André Deutsch, 1988). This is Shaffer's first version of the comedy; he soon revised it, particularly the ending, to remove the artillery attack against London buildings. All quotations to the play come from this edition, however, with page references noted parenthetically in my essay.

4. Michael Hinden argues that "the pain of incompleteness constitutes Shaffer's most profound and enduring theme" in "Trying to Like Shaffer," *Comparative Drama* 19, (Spring 1985): 14–29.

5. See my "'God-Hunting': The Chaos of Worship in *Equus* and *The Royal Hunt of the Sun*," *Modern Drama*, 21 (1978): 13–28; and "Peter Shaffer's *Amadeus* and *Shrivings*: God-Hunting Continued," *The Theatre Annual*, 39 (1984): 15–33.

6. In *Equus*, the human and Godly realms are most conflated: a square (the earth) is depicted within a circle (the divine). *The White Liars* and *Lettice and Lovage* explore suspended subterranean (or subconscious) realms where individuals escape from and arm themselves to face earthly destruction above.

7. Revealingly, Shaffer uses this metaphor in describing the reception of his "Battle of Shrivings"—the first version of what would become *Shrivings*: "Successful plays of large scope die for their authors

with a pleasant expiation, wrapped in a sheet of public approval: unsuccessful ones are apt to be left naked to the sky—particularly plays of turbulent nature—writhing under an obloquy which never quite covers them and so turns into oblivion" (from *Collected Plays*, 316).

8. Brian Connell, p. 7.

9. In *The Royal Hunt of the Sun*, Pizarro offers similar transcendental musings: "I felt then that seawater and bird droppings, and the little pits in human flesh were all linked together for some great end right out of the net of words to catch. Not just my words, but anyone's" (271).

10. See William J. Sullivan's "Peter Shaffer's *Amadeus*: The Making and un-Making of the Fathers," *American Imago: A Psychoanalytic Journal for Culture, Science, and the Arts*, 45 (Spring 1988): 45–60 for a thorough discussion of the ambiguity of the gesture of embrace in that drama.

# THE SUN AND THE HORSE: PETER SHAFFER'S SEARCH FOR WORSHIP

## James R. Stacy

The stage grows dark. A giant gold medallion looming upstage begins to glow. Chants of "Inca! Inca!" mix with exotic music. The medallion opens into a huge sun, extending twelve golden rays and revealing in its center Atahuallpa, sovereign Inca of Peru, Son of the Sun, Son of the Moon, Lord of the Four Quarters. The High Priests and the court, masked and robed in terra-cotta, prostrate themselves before their god-king. The play is Peter Shaffer's *The Royal Hunt of the Sun* (1964).[1]

Ten years later on another stage, the lights dim. Five men in metallic, skeletal horse masks stomp their cothurnus-like hooves on the floor as the "Equus Noise," an eerie humming, fills the theatre. A teenage boy ritualistically prepares one of the horses for a night ride, decking the animal-god with "sandals of majesty" and his "chinkle-chankle." After more ceremony the boy rides the horse into worshipful, sexual ecstasy. It is Shaffer's latest play, *Equus* (1974).[2]

In both plays Shaffer enters into the world of magic and ritual, primitivism and religious passion, in search of worship. In 1965 he wrote of *The Royal Hunt*, "It represents the sort of theatre I have long dreamed of creating, involving not only words but also mimes, masks, and magics; a ceremony to be ultimately created by the audience, whose task it will be to create for themselves . . . the fantastic apparition of the pre-Columbian world, and the terrible magnificence of the Conquistadors."[3] Later he came to realize that many people viewed the ritualistic, religious mystery of *The Royal Hunt* in terms of past history, "as though it had nothing to do with them today, as though it were some sort of . . . *outing*."[4] Thus, in *Equus* Shaffer brings "the numinous, . . . the things that throw shadows longer than themselves" into a contemporary, more clearly relevant setting, but he still seeks to "conjure the same dark forces as in *The Royal Hunt of the Sun*."[5] These dark forces lead Shaffer and his characters away from the emptiness of conventional societies and religions into deeper, primitive spiritual concerns.

Critics have focused upon many elements in Shaffer's rich plays, but often have overlooked or slighted the poet's exploration of man's spiritual needs. They regard *The Royal Hunt* as a play thematically about honor, greed, comradeship, or the meeting of two divergent cultures; certainly Shaffer considers all of these ideas in his play but not as the central theme. Some critics view *Equus* as a play about the right of society to "tamper with what is unique about an individual"[6] or as a defense of insanity.[7] *Equus* has also upset many psychiatrists who think the playwright maligns their profession. Psychiatrist Sanford Gifford accuses Shaffer of pandering to audiences by mixing "truth, banality and pretension" in order to "gratify our universal fantasies about our therapists."[8] Others see *Equus* as "an overblown closet-homosexual drama, in which the stable represents something like the Continental Baths and the horses six head of rough trade."[9] A homosexual element has also been identified by Robert Brustein in *The Royal Hunt*, in the relationship between Pizarro and Atahuallpa.[10] Psychiatrist Jules Glenn suggests that that relationship and the one between Martin Dysart and Alan Strang in *Equus* reflect "the disguised manifestations of twinship" between Shaffer and his brother Anthony, the author of *Sleuth*.[11] Amid such controversy of interpretation, especially in the case of *Equus*, it is easy to see how Shaffer's original intent—to explore the numinous—has become blurred as the central focus of these two works. By comparing *The Royal Hunt* and *Equus*, their common theme of man's need for worship can be illuminated more clearly.

Shaffer likely would agree with the critic who writes that "modern theatre, like modern religion, is by and large a tepid affair."[12] His solution for both problems is a return to the primitive. In order to revitalize the theatrical experience, Shaffer turns to visual and aural spectacle with its roots in ancient theatre and pagan ritual; thus an important element of his form supports his theme. He seeks an experience that is totally theatrical, "that is gestural as well as verbal, hallucinatory as well as cerebral—*magical*, if that word isn't now too debased to use."[13] Oscar Brockett notes in ancient ritual and theatre the common use of music, vocal sounds other than dialogue (chants), mime, masks, and costumes.[14] Most of these are also listed by anthropologist Anthony F. C. Wallace as among the "minimal categories of religious behavior."[15] All of these elements exist in both of the Shaffer plays.

In *The Royal Hunt* Shaffer lists twenty-one exotically orchestrated musical pieces, including "Toil Song," "The Massacre," and "Little Finch," which play integral parts in the play. Tropical bird cries are indicated throughout the script for mood and to accent dramatic moments. The music of *Equus* is not as melodic or alluring. Shaffer explains the Equus noise as a "choric effect . . . composed of humming, thumping and stamping—though never of neighing and whinnying. This noise heralds or illustrates the presence of Equus the God" (*Eq.* xv).[16] In *The Royal Hunt* chants are used by the Incas to salute Atahuallpa. Prayers are sung; a bitter lament is intoned. The king's order for his people to bring gold is a spoken lyric: "Bring him the gold of Cuzco and Coricancha! . . . Bring him the gold of Colae! Of Aymaraes and Arequipa! Bring him the gold of Chinu!" (*TRH* II, iii, 89). In *Equus* Shaffer makes chant-like use of biblical passages and of the genealogy which Alan has composed: "Prince begat Prance. And Prance begat Prankus! . . . And Neckwus begat Fleckwus, the King of Spit. And Fleckwus spoke out of his chinkle-chankle!" (*Eq.* I, xiv, 37).

In addition to the aural effects, mime gives *The Royal Hunt* some of its most theatrically exciting moments: the Mime of the Great Ascent, the Mime of the Great Massacre, the Gold Procession, and the Rape of the Sun. John Gassner viewed the mimed mountain climb of Pizarro and his conquistadors as "a tense theatrical experience."[17] Of the Rape of the Sun, Walter Kerr writes, "To watch the gold of the Inca empire being torn loose from its majestic moorings—a giant sunburst of daggers is greedily dismantled before our eyes—is to be faintly sickened. The language of the play has less impact than the boldly literal image."[18] In *Equus* Alan mimes a slave ritual before the picture of his god Equus, bridling himself with an invisible string and thrashing himself with an unseen coathanger. Mime is used in Alan's riding and grooming of the horses and in his handling of the hoof-pick with which he blinds them.

Both plays make use of minimal sets, depending on masks, costumes, and lights for striking visual imagery. John McClain of the *New York Journal American* describes the New York production of *The Royal Hunt*: "The entire play is performed on a circular platform with a single column in the middle which displays a large tribal emblem. Myriad lights project from above the stage area and the close sides of the proscenium, and the costumes of the Incas, some comprising elaborate festoons of feathers and most of the characters faceless in gilded masks, leave the scope and detail to the imagination of the audience."[19] The masked and hooved horses of *Equus* provide similarly striking figures against a simple single set, lending "an eerie, pre-Christian, totemistic air" to the play.[20] Bleacher seating is provided on the Plymouth Theatre stage for part of the audience and nonparticipating actors, thus increasing the union of spectator and performer and representing an arena for the ritualistic contest that takes place. In using all these elements of spectacle, Shaffer attempts to illuminate more meaningful dimensions of the theatrical experience and restore the theatre as a temple of magic and ritual.

Of even more importance to Shaffer than the physical enactment of ritual is the primitive impulse to create worship, a need that is increasingly unsatisfied in modern man. In both plays he is in search of what can reignite man's spiritual nature, what can transport "the commonplace religion we recognize to a dizzying ground where religion is a matter of passion," as one critic writes.[21] In his belief in civilization as a corrupter and his romantic idealization of the pagan, Shaffer seems similar to Rousseau, Audiberti, and Artaud.[22] Ionesco has said of himself that he is "desperate at not having some faith or other."[23] Shaffer has transferred such desperation to the characters of Pizarro and Dysart, who are both without worship in a sterile, materialistic world.

Of *The Royal Hunt* Shaffer writes that the underlying theme is "the search for God, the search for a definition of the idea of God."[24] In *Equus* he sends Dysart in search of that definition also: "Life is only comprehensible through a thousand local Gods. And not just the old dead ones with names like Zeus—no, but living Geniuses of Place and Person! . . . 'Worship as many as you can see—and more will appear!'" (*Eq.* I, xviii, 49). This idea of a multiplicity of gods is central to Shaffer's concept of worship. To him, organized society, with its governments, industries and churches, is necessarily restrictive, and detrimentally so. He writes, "To me the greatest tragic factor in History is man's apparent need to mark the intensity of his reaction to life by joining a band. For a band, to give definition, must find a rival or an enemy."[25] Thus, he has Pizarro lash out at an officer who refers to his army as "Pizarro's boys":

> Ah, the old band. The dear old regiment. Fool! Look, you were born a man. Not a Blue man, or a Green man, but A MAN. You are able to feel a thousand separate loves unordered by fear or solitude. Are you going to trade them all in for Gang-love? Flag-love? Carlos-the-Fifth-love? Jesus-the-Christ-love? All that has been tied on you; it is only this that makes you bay for death. (*TRH* II, x, 127)

Man should not limit himself to a worship defined by a band; he must individualize a worship and seek as many gods as he can. In the same way he should not limit himself to a single, consistent identity, which becomes nothing more than a category of social expectations. Shaffer has come to accept that contradictions and varying images are a truthful reflection of self.[26] For him there are many gods and many selves, and no band can embrace them all.

As a reflection of his distaste for bands, neither Shaffer nor his characters are satisfied by contemporary religions. He is distressed by the way man "canalizes the greatness of his spiritual awareness into the second-rate formula of a Church—any church: how he *settles* for a Church or Shrine or Synagogue; how he demands a voice, a law, an oracle, and over and over again puts into the hands of other men the reins of repression and the whip of Sole Interpretation."[27] He writes, "I resent deeply all churches. I despise them. No church or synagogue has ever failed to misuse its power."[28]

According to Shaffer, "the neurotic allegiances of Europe, the Churches and flags, the armies and parties, are villains of *The Royal Hunt of the Sun*."[29] The Spanish clergymen are narrow-minded men of hypcrisy, greed, and brutality. They exploit "heathens" for material gain and force Christian "salvation" upon them. When they encounter the Incas, Chaplain Valverde and the Franciscan friar DeNizza regard Peru as the land of the Anti-Christ. Valverde thinks so because Atahuallpa claims to be God; DeNizza, because he finds their tightly structured social system repulsive: it deprives them of their right to hunger and suffering. Pizarro castigates DeNizza for the priest's arrogance in believing that there is neither salvation nor love outside the Catholic Church. The old soldier gives a down-to-earth expression of Shaffer's attitude toward churches: "Dungballs to all churches that are or ever could be! How I hate you" (*TRH* II, x, 125).

Likewise, but neither as obviously nor as unsympathetically, the religious conventionalist in *Equus*—Mrs. Strang, the boy's mother—represents an undesirable position. Shaffer does not seem to judge her or distort her into a hypocritical zealot; instead he shows her as loving and well-intentioned, though misguided. Somehow parental dominance is easier for Shaffer to accept than that of the church. He writes: "I was born Jewish—though how a child can be born into any religion I don't see. You can only be born the child of your parents—not a Jew or a Christian. That's imposed upon you. It's a strange and sad thing that you have to spend so much time unlearning the damaging things you were taught—in all good faith on the part of your parents—as a child."[30] Nonetheless the damage is done, and in the case of Alan Strang his familial confusion over religion is one of the crucial factors in driving him into an unconventional worship and in producing the guilt that leads him to destroy his God. Mr. Strang, an avowed atheist, blames his wife's nightly reading of the Bible to Alan for the boy's crime of blinding the horses:

> A boy spends night after night having this stuff read into him: an innocent man tortured to death—thorns driven into his head—nails into his hands—a spear, jammed through his ribs. It can mark anyone for life, that kind of thing. . . . Bloody religion—it's our only real problem in this house. . . . (*Eq.* I, vii, 19)

Dysart learns of Alan's self-flagellating ritual before a photograph of a horse, a photograph which replaced a picture of Christ that even Mrs.

Strang admits was "a little extreme. The Christ was loaded down with chains, and the centurions were really laying on the stripes" (*Eq.*, I, xi, 30). The suffering Christ obviously inspired Alan's self-flagellation; in fact, "mortification of the flesh by pain" is considered to be a possible element of religious behavior.[31] In one of Shaffer's most well-crafted and emotionally revealing speeches, Mrs. Strang tells the psychiatrist why she thinks Alan committed the crime:

> But if you knew God, Doctor, you would know about the Devil. You'd know the Devil isn't made by what mummy says and daddy says. The Devil's *there*. It's an old-fashioned word, but a true thing. . . . I only know he was my little Alan, and then the Devil came. (*Eq.* II, xxiii, 66–67)

In both plays conventional religions not only fail to provide adequate spiritual fulfillment; they also act negatively to defeat or distort the spirit of the primitives.

In *The Royal Hunt* Martin serves as an intermediary figure, a religious conventionalist (one more idealistic than the clergymen, to be sure) who becomes a nonbeliever. Because Martin is presented in his youth and old age, he represents Pizarro (and Dysart) before and after disillusionment. Old Martin admits that in the beginning Pizarro was "my altar, my bright image of salvation. Time was when I'd have died for him, or for any worship" (*TRH* I, i, 17). Pizarro warns Young Martin against his idealism and his loyalty: "You're a worshipper, Martin. A groveller. You were born with feet but you prefer your knees. It's you who makes Bishops—Kings—Generals" (*TRH* I, v, 41). Thus Martin is a member of the band, but unlike Shaffer's other religious conventionalists (Mrs. Strang, Valverde, DeNizza), he is corrupted by his experience and loses faith. After Pizarro backs down on his promise to Atahuallpa to free him, Martin goes out into the night and "dropped my first tears as a man. My first and last. That was my first and last worship too. Devotion never came again" (*TRH* II, vii, 114). Thus Martin becomes a worshipless figure like his former idol, Pizarro, and like Dysart.

These nonbelievers, Pizarro and Dysart, in their relationships with the religious primitives Atahuallpa and Alan, are Shaffer's central concern in probing spiritual life apart from the band. Each primitive is an ardent believer, a worshipper, a potential savior, a passionate being with meaning in his existence; each nonbeliever is a cynic, an atheist, an empty being with no hope. In another parallel the atheists are the keepers; the worshippers, the prisoners. The former are reluctant conquerors; the latter, the conquered.

Many specific parallels can be drawn between Pizarro and Dysart, especially with respect to the emptiness of their lives. Shaffer writes of Pizarro, "He too is without joy. . . . For him, the savor of salt has been lost—lost through a lifetime of (to me, correct) rejections: flag, sword, Cross."[32] The sixty-three-year-old Pizarro tells DeSoto that life was once "fierce with feeling. Swords shone and armor sang, and cheese bit you, and kissing burned and Death—ah, death was going to make an exception in my case" (*TRH* I, x, 63). But once he realized the inevitability of death, he felt cheated and his soul became "frostbitten." He makes his most telling confession to Young Martin: "You own everything I've lost. I despise the keeping, and I loathe the losing. Where can a man live, between two hates?" (*TRH* I, v, 41). Pizarro is in an existential limbo of despair.

Shaffer develops Dysart as another frostbitten soul; like Pizarro his basic life force, his "horsepower," is too little (*Eq.* I, i, 2). Early in *Equus* Dysart diagnoses his doubts about the worth of psychiatry as comprising a "professional menopause" and laments that his job is "unworthy to fill me" (*Eq.* I, vi, 10). The barrenness of his life is further reflected in his marriage. He and his wife do not understand each other; they did not "go in for children"; they have not kissed in six years. Their marriage has become a matter of "antiseptic proficiency." Most disappointing to Dysart is that his wife does not share his love for Greek culture. He accuses her of being "utterly worshipless" (*Eq.* I, xviii, 49), but admits that he too is without any real worship: "Without worship you shrink, it's as brutal as that. . . . I shrank my *own* life" (*Eq.* II, xxv, 70). He also admits his sexual impotence and realizes that his annual "surrenders to the primitive" during his visits to Greece are a farce, "pallid and provincial" like his life, not pagan (*Eq.* II, xxv, 71).

Shaffer's primitives, Atahuallpa and Alan Strang, and their worships are similarly parallel. Looking at the objects of their worship, one notes a common paganism, for both the horse and the sun have long histories in mythology and ancient religions. In the plays the worship objects assume reverberating metaphorical meanings. In *Equus* the horse is endowed with a spiritual essence which Brendan Gill of *The New Yorker* terms "horseness," comparable to the concept of humanity. Thus, "horseness" is "separate from the life and death of individual horses and well worth our reverence; we violate it at our peril, as we violate our humanity at our peril."[33] Comparing Shaffer's use of the horse to D. H. Lawrence's, Jack Kroll of *Newsweek* sees the horse as representing, in Freudian terms, the power and danger of the unsublimated instincts.[34] The playwright himself says he uses the horse to take the audience back "to a time when there wasn't much distinction between the human and the animal."[35] This concept of horseness fascinates Dysart as he metaphysically muses, "Is it possible, at certain moments we cannot imagine, a horse can add its sufferings together—the non-stop jerks and jabs that are its daily life—and turn them into grief?" (*Eq.* II, xxii, 63). Although he yearns to, Dysart finally cannot accept the separate reality of horseness. If he were able to believe in it, then he too could become a primitive.

Likewise, if Pizarro could fully rekindle his childhood fascination for the sun and accept even further the "sun-ness" of Atahuallpa's belief, he too could find a worship. Pizarro recalls that as a youth he thought if he could find the place where the sun sets, he would find the source of life there. "I myself can't fix anything nearer to a thought of worship than standing at dawn and watching it fill the world," he says (*TRH* I, x, 65). After his acquaintance with Atahuallpa, Pizarro becomes even more absorbed by the idea of the sun as an active God:

> What else is a God but what we know we can't do
> without? The flowers that worship it, the sunflowers in
> their soil, are us after night, after cold and lightless days,
> turning our faces to it, adoring. The sun is the only God I
> know! We eat you to walk! We drink you to sing. (*TRH*
> II, xi, 132)

Pizarro stakes his final hope on the sun to resurrect Atahuallpa, but he is cruelly disappointed.

Both forms of worship in the plays make use of common Christian motifs, resurrection being the most prominent one in *The*

*Royal Hunt.* Atahuallpa explains to Pizarro the traditional belief of the Incas that no one but his father, the Sun, can take his life: "If you kill me tonight I will rise at dawn when my Father first touches my body with light" (*TRH* II, xi, 130). Incans also have their own style of confession. The use of Christian themes in *Equus* obviously stems from Alan's childhood training. He prepares a biblical genealogy for Equus, "so-and-so begat," ending in "Behold—I give you Equus, my only begotten son!" (*Eq.* I, xiv, 37). Elements of Alan's riding ritual find parallels in Christian belief, including the "place of Ha Ha" (from the Book of Job), the Ark of the Manbit, and a Last Supper of sugar lumps. Alan apparently derived the concept of "becoming one" with Equus from something his mother told him: "When Christian cavalry first appeared in the New World, the pagans thought horse and rider was one person" (*Eq.* I, vii, 15). (One may note the possible confusion in a child's mind and imagination between the words *cavalry* and *Calvary*.) The concept of "becoming one" can also be related to the mystical concepts of the Holy Trinity as one God, man's union with God in death, and man and woman's becoming one in marriage.

Of equal importance is the sexual nature of Alan's becoming one with Equus, as revealed in his climactic ride in Act I: "I'm stiff! Stiff in the wind! . . . *I'm raw! Raw!* Feel me on you! . . . I want to be *in* you! I want to BE you forever and ever!—*Equus, I love you!* . . . Make us One Person! *One Person!* " (*Eq.* I, xxi, 62). Certainly the ride and the relationship are of a sexual nature, but looking beyond the physical aspects of sex, one may view the interrelation of sex and religion as an historical fact. Primitive man regarded sexual reproduction as "the deepest and most awe-inspiring attribute of nature,"[36] and more practically he recognized that fertility was responsible for his own birth, the birth of his offspring, and for plentiful crops and herds to feed and clothe them.[37] Because sex was a great mystery and a great necessity, it became the central focus of the dawnings of religious thought. Anthropologist O. A. Wall writes, "All religions are based on sex; some, like the ancient Egyptian, Greek, and Roman, or the modern Brahmanis worship of Siva, very coarsely so, according to modern civilized thought; others, like the Christian religion, more obscurely so."[38] Wall further observes, "In its origin, the worship of sex was pure *in intent* and as far removed from any idea of anything unclean or obscene as any of our own religions."[39] H. Cutner, a British anthropologist, contends that in the process of civilization, the religious-sexual functions and feelings of primitive man have been idealized into what, for some, is more properly called love.[40] Whether idealized as love or accepted as sex, the instinct for union is "the greatest fact in human experience, the source of life and of nearly all its deepest emotions; the wellspring of our intensest pleasures as well as of our deepest griefs."[41] It is in this light that sex becomes an important element in Shaffer's plays.

In addition to the eroticism of Alan's midnight rides on Equus, Shaffer presents the boy at a moment of sexual crisis, torn by his devotion to Equus, his mother's strict morals, his discovery about his father's sexual needs, and his own adolescent longing for intercourse with Jill. The sexual feelings expressed in *The Royal Hunt* are also intense, but they are neither as important nor as obvious as they are in *Equus*. Pizarro recalls that the best hour of his life was spent when he lay with a girl by the sea "wrapped up in her against the cold" (*TRH* I, x, 63). He loved women with "all the juice" in him, but eventually he felt cheated by them, as he did by all life and time. Shaffer's intention in both plays, particularly in *Equus*, is to use sex as a passion with which his audience can readily identify, and to seek an even more transcendent, more intense, and more meaningful passion in religion—the anthropological origins of which are inextricably linked with sex.

The plays also share a concern for the concept of God as slave: "man creates God in order to enslave him," in both *The Royal Hunt* and *Equus*.[42] Atahuallpa, the God, is a master who commands the strict obedience of his subjects, setting for them a pattern of life they unquestioningly follow. In a reversal of roles he becomes Pizarro's prisoner and slave when he is bound arm to arm by a rope, initially as a means of protecting the Inca's life. But as his despair and confusion increase, Pizarro makes a slave puppet of Atahuallpa: "I've got the Sun on a string!" (*TRH* II, xi, 132).

In *Equus* Alan is also a prisoner, sentenced to the hospital by a court, but the concept of God as slave is primarily expressed in his view of the harnessed (enchained) Equus. As he begins his ride in Act I, he tells Dysart, "The King rides out on Equus, mightiest of horses. Only I can ride him. . . . Equus, my Godslave!" (*Eq.* I, xxi, 61). The interconnection of the slave/master roles is revealed by Dysart who says to Alan, "He lives *one hour* every three weeks—howling in a mist. And after the service kneels to a slave who stands over him obviously and unthrowably his master. With my body I thee worship" (*Eq.* II, xxv, 69). The slave/master paradox takes on psychological as well as religious implications when one considers Freud's comparison of the ego (the Apollonian, Dysart) and the id (the Dionysian, Alan) to a rider and his horse: "The horse provides the locomotive energy and the rider has the prerogative of determining the goal and of guiding the movements of his powerful mount towards it. But all too often in the relationship between the ego and the id we find a picture of the less ideal situation in which the rider is obliged to guide his horse in the direction in which it itself wants to go."[43] Ultimately Equus shows himself to be such a self-determining master, for Alan is unable to function sexually with a girl: "When I touch her, I felt *Him*. . . . When I shut my eyes, I saw Him at once" (*Eq.* II, xxxiii, 91–92). To alleviate the guilt, Alan blinds his jealous, all-seeing God.

Motifs of blindness and eyesight, light and dark, occur in *The Royal Hunt* as well as in *Equus*. Pizarro dreams of "a black king with glowing eyes" (*TRH* I, x, 66). God's eyes are regarded as capable of blinding and killing. In his final despair after Atahuallpa's death, Pizarro says, "You have no eyes for me now, Atahuallpa: they are dusty balls of amber I can tap on." And he cries out, "I die between two darks: blind eyes and a blind sky"(*TRH* II, xii, 137). Ironically, Pizarro the conqueror is in the dark; Atahuallpa the conquered is basked by the light of his father, the Sun. Expressing the paradox of these motifs, in his introduction to *The Royal Hunt*, Shaffer quotes Genet: "To see the soul of a man is to be blinded by the sun" (*TRH*, p. ix).

In *Equus* the significance of seeing is established prior to Alan's reenactment of blinding the six horses. From his mother during childhood, Alan learned, "God sees you, Alan. God's got eyes everywhere" (*Eq.* I, xi, 31). When Alan tries to have sex with Jill, whose eyes fascinate him, his guilt is inflamed by the idea that the horses have seen everything. He sees their rolling eyes and then grabs a hoof-pick to blind them and absolve himself from their accusing stares (*Eq.* II, xxv, 94). Like Pizarro, the disillusioned Dysart ends the play in spiritual darkness: "I stand in the dark with a pick in my hand, striking at heads! I need . . . a way of seeing in the dark. What way is this? *What dark is this?* " (*Eq.* II, xxv, 98–99).

The crux of Shaffer's exploration into these worships is in the admiration the nonbelievers develop for their primitives. Both Pizarro and Dysart initially take a professional interest in their adversaries as military opponent or as patient, but they quickly sense something fateful and unsettling about them. Of all those Pizarro has waged war on, Atahuallpa is special: "Of all the meetings I have made in my life, this with him is the one I have to make. Maybe it's my death. Or maybe new life. I feel just this. All my days have been a path to this one morning" (*TRH* I, x, 66). In *Equus* Dysart also feels a specialness about Alan, who becomes "a last straw, a last symbol" for the psychiatrist (*Eq.* I, ii, 3). Hesther, the magistrate who brings Alan to the hospital, warns Dysart that the boy has "vibrations" which are "quite startling" (*Eq.* I, ii, 4–5). Dysart soon must agree that Alan "has the strangest stare I ever met" (*Eq.* I, vi, 10), and he realizes that "treating him is going to be unsettling." The night after their first meeting, Dysart dreams that he butchers five-hundred children; it is Alan's face on "every victim across the stone" (*Eq.* I, vi, 10). The captors' fascination with their prisoners continues to grow.

As they are bargaining for gold, Pizarro finally admits his attraction for Atahuallpa: "He has some meaning for me, this Man-God. An immortal man in whom all his people live completely. He has an answer for time" (*TRH* II, iii, 88). Dysart finds that Alan also has meaning for him. He confesses to Hesther, "That boy has known a passion more ferocious than I have felt in any second of my life. And let me tell you something: I envy it" (*Eq.* II, xxv, 70). He continues, "I sit looking at pages of centaurs tramping the soil of Argos—and outside my window he is trying to *become one*, in a Hampshire field!" (*Eq.* II, xxv, 71). Dysart translates the meaning of Alan's stare into a very concrete challenge: "At least I galloped: When did you?" (*Eq.* II, xxv, 70).

Pizarro and Dysart face the same moral dilemma: Do I fulfill my professional duty—the killing of Atahuallpa, the curing of Alan Strang? Or do I betray the band and allow my primitive his worship? What are my choices? If not their own unique worships, then what? Shaffer does not pretend that either worship is perfect. Atahuallpa's way ultimately denies his people of free will, although, like the inhabitants of B. F. Skinner's Walden II, they seem to find happiness in what has been predetermined for them. Alan's worship is marred on a literal level by its bestiality, which offends societal mores, and by the violence to which the boy is driven in struggling to resolve the conflict of his religious and social instincts. Shaffer is not evangelizing specifically for either the Sun or the Horse; rather, the attraction of the worships lies in the intensity with which they are pursued. Such passionate intensity is preferable to the lackluster existence of Pizarro and Dysart. Pizarro sees that the worship the Inca offers his people is better than that of the Europeans: "If I go marketing for Gods, what do I buy? The God of Europe with all its death and blooding, or Atahuallpa of Peru? His spirit keeps an Empire sweet and still as corn in the field" (*TRH* II, x, 126).

The alternative to Horse worship is no more appealing than the alternative to Sun worship. Dysart comes to see that Equus is the core of Alan's life. The boy has nothing else: no interest in literature, science, art, music, history; no friends. "He's a modern citizen for whom society doesn't exist," Dysart says (*Eq.* II, xxv, 69). The psychiatrist questions the magistrate's desire to return Alan to a normal life: "You mean a normal boy has one head; a normal head has two ears?" He sees the normal as "the dead stare in a million adults. . . . It is the Ordinary made beautiful; it is also the Average made lethal. The Normal is the indispensable, murderous God of Health. . ." (*Eq.* I., xix, 50–51). If Alan is in pain, as Hesther claims he is, at least it is "his pain, he made it, it is unique to him" (*Eq.* II, xxv, 70). The normal world offers him only mini-scooters, multi-lane highways, plastics, factories, smirky sex, and an "abstract and unifying God" (*Eq.* II, xxxv, 98). Neither alternative to the primitives' worships is satisfying, but reality dictates that a choice be made.

So they choose. Because they refuse to surrender their professional identities, they must destroy their captives. Shaffer has raised the hopes of his audience by making Pizarro and Dysart so intensely involved with, and apparently enlightened by, their primitives that the men seem ready to desert the band. But finally Shaffer denies those hopes with the respective cruel realities of killing and curing. Because the playwright fails to provide the precise moments of decision for Pizarro and Dysart, moments in which they clearly reaffirm their allegiance to the band or accept their defeat by it, Shaffer leaves himself open to charges of faulty motivation. It has been suggested that structural demands rather than characterization predetermine Dysart's decision to go through with Alan's cure; that if Dysart had decided not to cure Alan, Shaffer would have been left without an ending scene for his second act to parallel Alan's climactic ride on Equus at the end of Act I.[44] In a similar manner, an external motivation can be posited for Pizarro's decision to kill Atahuallpa: history. Although certainly not confining himself to historical details in *The Royal Hunt*, Shaffer at least seems to be tied to the authenticity of the results of the Conquest. Pizarro did not intervene. Atahuallpa was killed. He was not resurrected.

Although the decisions of Pizarro and Dysart may be disappointing and unclearly established, they are not unlikely given the basic weakness of the men and the overriding strength of the band. Distinct moments of decision might have clarified their motivations, but such precision might also have been inconsistent with the nature of Shaffer's desperate and confused characters. Although they do not admit defeat to the band before their acts of destruction, they do realize that defeat afterwards. They know that their births and their experiences lock them in, that they are "all reined up in old languages and old assumptions" (*Eq.* I, i, 2). The band, not structural or historical needs, has finally robbed Shaffer's characters of free will. Thus bound, Pizarro is unwilling to sacrifice the lives of his one hundred sixty-five men in order to save the life of Atahuallpa, the only person of spiritual value he has ever revered, and to prevent the enslavement and exploitation of an entire empire of twenty-four million. His sense of military duty and reputation prevents him from deserting his men; thus, he awaits a miracle which he can only hope for, not believe in: the resurrection of Atahuallpa. In a like manner, Dysart will not give up certainty of routine and material comfort; he cannot escape his "eternal timidity" (*Eq.* II, xxv, 70). Although he questions his curing of Alan, he goes through with it. If either nonbeliever had deserted his professional identity, he could have fled into a new spiritual life—Pizarro seeking the resting place of the Sun high in the Andes, Dysart searching for centaurs in the plains of Argos. Such romantic quests would inevitably end in failure, even death, for the sun is in space and there are no centaurs. But perhaps those days of search would bring the spiritual fulfillment—life rather than mere existence, no matter how temporary—both men are seeking. Conventional lives have not provided them with answers; they have served only to make the men unable to "jump clean-hoofed on to a whole new track of being" which they are not even sure is there (*Eq.* I, i, 2).

The choices made, the worships end. As a final blow to the spirit of Atahuallpa, Pizarro convinces him to be baptized a Christian so that he will not be burned but hanged, thereby keeping his body in one piece for resurrection. As the sun rises the next day, Pizarro and the Inca nation await Atahuallpa's resurrection. Chanting, masked Incans slowly leave the stage when the rays of the dawning sun fail to bring their God back to life. Pizarro is left alone with Atahuallpa's body, which he contemplates. Suddenly and viciously he slaps it and shouts, "Cheat! You've cheated me!" (*TRH* II, xii, 137). It is his "last and greatest disillusionment." [45] Old Martin says of him, "He sat down that morning and never really got up again" (*TRH* II, xii, 138).

If Atahuallpa becomes a corpse, then Alan Strang becomes a ghost. The Inca dies literally, the boy spiritually; neither is resurrected. The Sun does not come to save Atahuallpa, and Equus gallops off with Alan's "intestines in his teeth" (*Eq.* II, xxxv, 97). Sadly, angrily, Dysart realizes that he has destroyed Alan's passion, his personal pain: "You won't gallop any more, Alan. Horses will be quite safe. . . . You will, however, be without pain. More or less completely without pain" (*Eq.* II, xxxv, 98). Dysart is left, like Pizarro, hovering over the stripped body of the worshipper he inexplicably revered and reluctantly destroyed. The echoes of Equus fill the room as he laments the "irreversible, terminal things" done there. Just as Pizarro sat down and never got up again, so Dysart admits, "There is now, in my mouth, this sharp chain. And it never comes out" (*Eq.* II, xxxv, 99).

Neither of Shaffer's nonbelievers finds the meaning he is seeking, but in his search he has glimpsed the shadow world of the soul. In these searches Shaffer aims to arouse in his audience the same doubts and send them looking for new meaning. In the spectacle of *The Royal Hunt* and *Equus* he attempts to make the theatrical experience a total, ritualistic involvement of the senses, the mind, and the spirit. He discounts conventional religions and other bands as detrimental because they lock men into predetermined, structured worships and lives without regard to the reality of self: the multiplicity of self, which demands a multiplicity of gods. The products of modern churches are of two kinds: the conventional believer with the wrong answers (Valverde, DeNizza, Mrs. Strang) and the nonbelievers with no answers (Pizarro, Dysart). When new answers arise from passionate, primitive worshippers (Atahuallpa, Alan Strang), the spirits of Shaffer's nonbelievers flare up with the hope that they have found an answer, a god, a worship. But the band is too much with them, and they destroy the worshippers along with their hope. Once again sadly immobile in his life, Pizarro sits and watches the sun "roam uncaught over an empty pasture." And Dysart now and always feels the sharp pain of his confinement to convention, as Equus gallops back into the shadows of the spirit.

# Notes

1. Peter Shaffer, *The Royal Hunt of the Sun* (New York: Stein and Day, 1966), p. 32.

2. Shaffer, *Equus* (New York: Avon Books, 1974), pp. 56–62.

3. Shaffer, "'To See the Soul of a Man . . . ,'" *New York Times*, 24 October 1965, Sec. 2, p. 3.

4. Quoted in Tom Buckley, " 'Write Me,' Said the Play to Peter Shaffer," *New York Times Magazine*, 13 April 1975, p. 20.

5. Ibid.

6. Albert E. Kalson, Review of *Equus*, *ETJ*, 25 (December 1973): 515.

7. John Simon, "The Blindness Is Within," *New York*, 11 November 1974, p. 118. Shaffer has been quoted as saying, "I do not believe that Art and insanity have anything to say to each other. The greatest Art—the symphonies of Haydn or the paintings of Bellini—virtually defines sanity for me" (quoted in Buckley, p. 38).

8. Sanford Gifford, "Psychoanalyst Says Nay to 'Equus,'" *New York Times*, 15 December 1974, pp. 1, 5.

9. Buckley, p. 28.

10. Robert Brustein, *The Third Theatre* (New York: Alfred A. Knopf, 1969), p. 115.

11. Quoted in Buckley, p. 32.

12. Howard Kissel, Review of *Equus, Women's Wear Daily*, 18 October 1974, in *New York Theatre Critics Reviews (NYTCR)*, 4 November 1974, p. 203.

13. Shaffer, "'To See the Soul of a Man. . . ,'" p. 3.

14. Oscar G. Brockett, *History of the Theatre* (Boston, 1974), pp. 2–6.

15. Anthony F. C. Wallace, *Religion: An Anthropological View* (New York, 1966), pp. 53–66.

16. Subsequent references to the scripts will be made as *Eq.* or *TRH*, act number, scene number, page number in previously cited publications of the plays.

17. John Gassner, "Broadway in Review," *ETJ* 18 (March 1966): 57.

18. Walter Kerr, Review of *The Royal Hunt of the Sun, New York Herald Tribune*, 27 October 1965, in *NYTCR*, 8 November 1965, p. 295.

19. John McClain, "Size, Style, and Talent," *New York Journal American*, October 1965, in *NYTCR*, 8 November 1965, p. 293.

20. Brendan Gill, "Unhorsed," *The New Yorker*, 4 November 1974, p. 123.

21. Kissel, p. 203.

22. Robert Brustein suggests that the idea of *The Royal Hunt* was derived from Artaud's *The Conquest of Mexico*, his first scenario for his projected Theatre of Cruelty. In the tableau Artaud sought to "correct 'the false conceptions the Occident has somehow formed concerning paganism and certain natural religions,' while dramatizing, in burning images, the destruction of Montezuma and his Aztecs by the armies of Cortez" (115).

23. Quoted in Ronald Hayman, *Eugene Ionesco* (London, 1972), p. 8.

24. Quoted in John Russell Taylor, *The Angry Theatre: New British Drama* (New York, 1969), p. 277.

25. Shaffer, "'To See the Soul of a Man . . . ,'" p. 3.

26. Buckley, p. 40.

27. Shaffer, "'To See the Soul of a Man . . . ,'" p. 3.

28. Quoted in Barbara Gelb, ". . . And Its Author," *New York Times*, 14 November 1965, Sec. 2, pp. 2, 4.

29. Shaffer, "'To See the Soul of a Man. . . ,'" p. 3.

30. Quoted in Gelb, p. 4.

31. Wallace, p. 55.

32. Shaffer, "'To See the Soul of a Man . . .,'" p. 3.

33. Gill, p. 123.

34. Jack Kroll, "Horse Power," *Newsweek*, 4 November 1974, p. 60.

35. Quoted in Buckley, p. 25.

36. O. A. Wall, *Sex and Sex Worship* (St. Louis, 1922), p. 377, quoting *The British Encyclopedia*.

37. H. Cutner, *A Short History of Sex Worship* (London, 1950), pp. 2–3.

38. Wall, p. 2.

39. Ibid., p. 378.

40. Cutner, p. 2.

41. Wall, p. 116.

42. Kalson, p. 514.

43. Quoted in the souvenir program for the British National Theatre's production of *Equus*, 1974.

44. Virginia Scott, personal correspondence, 20 February 1976.

45. Gassner, p. 58.

# STRADDLING A DUAL POETICS IN *AMADEUS:* SALIERI AS TRAGIC HERO AND JOKER

## Felicia Hardison Londré

It is not surprising that Peter Shaffer's *Amadeus* was especially popular in Eastern Bloc countries before the November 1989 breaching of the Berlin Wall. With only a slight change of emphasis, the play can serve as a historical variation on a story all too familiar in life: that of an original or courageous voice silenced by the authority of the state which had assumed the power to determine whose voices should be heard at all. Indeed, in the Leningrad production directed by Georgi Tovstonogov, Mozart's death was depicted with the Venticelli pointing their canes at him like rifles. When Ying Ruocheng staged the Chinese premiere of the play in Beijing in 1986, he commented obliquely, "The plays sheds a lot of light on some of the things the Chinese are constantly discussing these days: how to treat genius, or talent; how to deal with professional jealousy; what is the relationship between morals and ability."[1] Behind Ying's words lay bitter memories of the cultural Revolution, when the untalented actress who became Mao's wife suppressed all but eight state-approved Beijing Operas. East or west, the broad outlines of the story in *Amadeus* support the view that Mozart was a tragic victim and Salieri his oppressor. A dramaturgical analysis of the plot, however, corroborates the fact that Salieri also is the play's protagonist.

When Peter Shaffer chose to make Antonio Salieri the protagonist of *Amadeus*, he set himself a task as formidable as that of Shakespeare in arousing sympathy for Macbeth or Richard III. Asking a

*115*

modern audience to understand and forgive Salieri's professional jealousy of Mozart poses little problem, but inveigling the audience to side with Salieri in his consciously plotted undermining of Mozart's career and in his hastening of Mozart's death at thirty-five amounts to virtual sacrilege. Even Salieri is forced to admit that the music issuing from Mozart is "a voice of God," "an Absolute Beauty." Yet Salieri's overriding purpose throughout the scenes set in the eighteenth century is to suppress that voice; and his purpose in the frame story set thirty-two years later is to win posterity's understanding (and implicit approval) of that earlier action.

Shaffer recalls that when he started to write a play about Mozart and Salieri he "spent virtually a year attempting a different opening scene every week. It was an exceedingly hard task to find the center of the work—to reduce a mass of historical material to anything remotely coherent and yet dramatic."[2] His effort to achieve coherence must have meant following—consciously or unconsciously—the Aristotelian model of the elements of the drama. This was endemic to his theatrical formation and is evident in his earlier plays. However, Shaffer's attempt to force Salieri into the mold of "tragic hero" did not entirely succeed, although many of the elements are there. The magnitude of Salieri's story, which escalates to a declaration of war on God Himself, does encompass an action that is "both unified and complete" and is "capable of happening according to the rule of probability or necessity."[3] Aristotle's three elements of plot are also included in Salieri's story: *peripety* or reversal of fortune, *anagnorisis* or recognition, and suffering.

Yet there is a dramaturgical problem connected with each of these as they are worked out in *Amadeus*. From the audience's perspective, Salieri's *peripety* and *anagnorisis* occur at the same time, as Aristotle recommended, because they are juxtaposed in Salieri's final monologue, in his recounting of events. His recognition is signalled when he says, "And slowly I understood the nature of God's punishment," which was to grant Salieri exactly what he had asked: not musical brilliance, but Fame. Then, after "thirty years of being called 'distinguished' by people incapable of distinguishing," came Salieri's reversal: public indifference. Thus, in the context of the character's life, there is no connection at all between recognition and reversal; indeed, there is an unconventional chronological reversal in that the recognition did not grow out of a fall from fortune, but preceded it by three decades.

Furthermore, contrary to Aristotle's precepts, these developments are presented as narrative rather than as dramatic action (although they are illustrated pantomimically by the attitudes of the Citizens on stage). Even more problematic is the fact that Salieri is not changed as a result of his recognition. He announces his new-found awareness, but he does not feel it. He never admits to himself that he was at fault from the beginning, not only because he asked for the wrong thing, but because his end of the bargain with God was only superficially kept, even before Mozart arrived on the scene. Despite his vow to "live with virtue" and "to better the lot of [his] fellows," Salieri gave way to gluttony and gossip-mongering. His employment of the Venticelli reveals his preoccupation with jockeying for social position and professional advancement. The only hint of his "social virtue" comes after his declaration of war on God, when he tells the audience, "I went to the palace and resigned from all my committees to help the lot of poor musicians." His aid to poor musicians had not extended to Mozart, who was living in poverty even before Salieri fully appreciated the extent of the "obscene child's" musical genius and its potential threat to his own pre-eminence. Finally, he expresses no remorse for the evil course of action he followed as a result of his misconstruction of the original terms of his bargain with God.

After his moment of recognition, when he states that he understands God's punishment, Salieri is still driven to attempt to outsmart God. By spreading the rumor that he poisoned Mozart, he expects posterity to keep his name alive along with Mozart's. And, also driven to portray himself to posterity as the victim of an unjust God, Salieri attempts suicide. Both courses of action are thwarted. The public's disbelief of the rumor and failure of Salieri's attempted suicide finally bring about his first serious suffering; that is, the first suffering that comes as a consequence of his own actions as opposed to the pain of jealousy that served dramatically to motivate his earlier course of action. The suffering inflicted upon Salieri as "tragic hero," as one who dared to engage in battle against God, is curiously mitigated, indicated only by a stage direction: "Salieri lowers his head, conceding defeat."

Although Aristotle did not employ a term that would translate as "tragic hero," he did attempt to specify the kind of character who would be appropriate as the central figure in a tragedy: "a man who is neither a paragon of virture and justice nor undergoes the change to misfortune through any real badness or wickedness but because of some mistake [*hamartia* ] . . . of great weight and consequence" (38). He states further that tragic characters should be good ("their speech or their action reveals the moral quality of some choice"), appropriate, credible in terms of human nature in general, and consistent (43). Salieri fits the role in every respect save one. From a modern perspective, Salieri seriously falls short in the category of goodness. Within the world of the play, however, as C. J. Gianakaris has shown, Salieri is the "normative figure" in an orderly universe; he "epitomizes the 'standard' musical aesthetics of the time and the typical rational man of the Enlightenment."[4]

It might thus be said that the play exemplifies what Augusto Boal sees as one of five types of modifications to Aristotle's system "introduced by new societies."[5] Boal labels his fourth type of modification "Negative Hamartia Versus Negative Social Ethos," and explains that "the hamartia of the protagonist . . . displays an impressive collection of negative qualities, sins, errors, etc. On the other hand, the social ethos (that is, the moral tendencies, ethics) of society . . . is here entirely in agreement with the character" (43). Boal continues, "The author wishes to show a social ethics accepted by the society portrayed on stage, but he himself, the author, does not share that ethics, and proposes another. The universe of the work is one, and our universe, or at least our momentary position during the spectacle, is another" (44). Shaffer's own reverence for Mozart's work shines through in Salieri's appreciation for Mozart's musical "aberration," and equally transparent is Shaffer's repugnance toward the kind of society in which Salieri is enmeshed. However, instead of insisting upon the gulf between the world of the play and the ethos of our own time, Shaffer apparently attempts to reconcile them by creating a complicity between Salieri and the members of the theater audience, whom Salieri addresses directly as "Ghosts of the distant Future."

That complicity—which amounts to an intellectual appreciation of Salieri's efforts to assert himself as a representative of mankind fighting back, however underhandedly, against divine injustice—is not the same as the emotional involvement that comes with empathy. As defined by Boal, empathy—in Aristotle's "coercive system"—is "the emotional relationship which is established between the character and spectator and which provokes, fundamentally, a delegation of power on the part of the spectator, who becomes an object in relation to the character: whatever happens to the latter, happens vicariously to the spectator. . . . The only indispensable element in empathy is that the spectator assumes a 'passive' attitude, delegating his ability to act" (102). Shaffer may have wanted to achieve an empathic relationship between Salieri and the audience; certainly Salieri's through-line in the frame story has him working toward that end. Although Shaffer gives Salieri the advantages of direct address to the audience (including shameless winks, jokes, and pathetic appeals), a sophisticated wit, and a psychologically credible complexity, it is unlikely that very many audience members ever identify with Salieri's mediocrity in his chosen career or that they "delegate power" to him in his battle with God. As Ian McKellan noted, "what's difficult is the relation of Salieri with the audience. It is a non-stop operation. Salieri has long monologues and is constantly taking the audience into his confidence. I have to woo the audience."[6]

Salieri has to work hard to overcome the strong appeal of his nemesis, a figure "encased in three centuries of adulation" (Gianakaris 39), especially since the scenes in which the bumptiously boorish Mozart appears are dramatically the play's most effective. Mozart's cat-and-mouse game with Constanze, the scene of his spontaneous variations on Salieri's ceremonial march, his brilliant Act 2 monologue about the sounds of humanity ascending like music to God, all spark the action to higher levels of dramatic interest. Such surges of energy emanating from Mozart's presence in a scene, combined with a modern audience's predisposition to sympathize with that kind of social misfit who deflates authority figures, add to the challenge Shaffer faced in attempting to tip the emotional balance toward Mozart's opponent.

Since Shaffer could not rely upon an Aristotelian dramaturgy (even as modified by new societies) to achieve his goal, he seems to have borrowed—either consciously or intuitively—from another system. A number of congruities are evident between *Amadeus* and the poetics that Boal proposes in place of those of either Aristotle or Brecht. Boal's "poetics of the oppressed," or what he calls "the Joker system," takes as its main objective the transformation of spectators— who are normally passive beings in the theatrical phenomenon—into subjects, into agents of the dramatic action. This approach "focuses on the action itself: the spectator delegates no power to the character (or actor) either to act or to think in his place; on the contrary, he himself assumes the protagonic role, changes the dramatic action, tries out solutions, discusses plans for change—in short trains himself for real action. In this case, perhaps the theater is not revolutionary in itself, but it is surely a rehearsal for the revolution. The liberated spectator, as a whole person, launches into action. No matter that the action is fictional; what matters is that it is action!" (122). Fully realized, of course, Boal's poetics would liberate the theatrical experience from the pre-scripted dramatic text. But Boal describes how his Arena Theater of Sao Paulo was able to "nationalize" texts like Machiavelli's *Mandragola* and Molière's *Tartuffe*, making them responsive to the concerns of ordinary Brazilians, without changing a line of the original (163–164). Thus, the idea of *Amadeus* as a rehearsal for revolution is not so far-fetched, especially in view of the message it has communicated to Eastern Bloc peoples. Certainly, given Salieri's drive to win the audience's approval in the frame story, *Amadeus* grants the spectator a far more active role than do most plays in the European tradition. And, as previously indicated, Salieri's probable success at winning the audiences over to his view is not a foregone conclusion, even when the role is played by an actor of great charm.

Boal's "Joker" system is based upon several principles. First, it proposes to present both the play and its analysis within the same performance, focusing the action "according to a single, predetermined perspective" through the use of a "Joker" who offers "explanations" (175). According to Boal, it is necessary to move this figure "away from the other characters, to bring him close to the spectators" (175).

Such a function and position might well be ascribed to Salieri, who is sometimes regarded by critics as more of a "ringmaster" or "master of ceremonies" than as a full participant within the flashback story. Boal suggests that the Joker's explanations will "make the performance develop on two different and complementary levels: that of the fable (which can use all the conventional imaginative resources of the theater), and that of the 'lecture,' in which the 'Joker' becomes an exegete" (175). Clearly, *Amadeus* is well accommodated to this view. Secondly, the "Joker" system calls for stylistic variety. "Each chapter or episode can be treated in the manner that fits it best" (177), as overall unity is maintained by the Joker's "explanations." The stylistic variety of *Amadeus* is unquestionable; it purports to be a play of ideas, but Shaffer realized during the creative process that he was also writing a play with operatic elements: "Here was an opening chorus, the whispers of the populace. Here, with the entrance of the two gossipy courtiers, was a duet. Here is a trio, and later a quintet. Salieri's monologues are big arias. The play has the savor, the smell, and taste of an opera."[7]

*Amadeus* is also part historical drama, part melodrama, part vaudeville, and part music-appreciation course. And Salieri—as if to doubly justify his dramaturgical title of "Joker"—has been compared to a stand-up comedian. The third aesthetic basis for the system is the attempt "to resolve the option between the character-object and the character-subject which schematically derives from the belief that thought determines action or, on the contrary, that action determines thought. . . . The intent is to restore the full freedom of the character-subject within the strict outlines of social analysis" (178–179). In this regard, *Amadeus* remains ambiguous, for Salieri's actions do originate in the subjectivity of his character (as in Aristotelian tragedy), but there are also instances in which the dramatic action defines the character, as in Salieri's *omophagia*, when he tears off a corner of Mozart's music, elevates it like a communion host, places it on his tongue, chews it, and declares, "We are both poisoned, Amadeus. I with you: you with me" (552).

*Amadeus* corresponds most tellingly to Boal's "poetics of the oppressed" in his section on structures of the "Joker." Boal notes that in his system "the protagonist does not coincide necessarily with the main

character. In *Macbeth* it can be Macduff. . . . The character with whom
the author wishes to link empathically with the public performs the
protagonic function" (181). In *Amadeus*, this would clearly be Mozart,
who conforms to Boal's stricture that the "protagonic" character retain
his verisimilitude, his fictional reality, within the context of the play.
He does not "break character" or breach the play's established
conventions, even though the "Joker" might be simultaneously
analyzing some detail. The protagonic character functions, as Mozart
does, "to reconquer the empathy that is always lost every time a
performance tends toward a high degree of abstraction" (181). The
function of the "Joker," on the other hand, is to create or describe a
magical reality which must be accepted by all the other characters. His
outlook, like that of Salieri, is "assumed to be above and beyond that of
the other characters in time and space. . . . In this way, all the theatrical
possibilities are conferred upon the "joker" function: he is magical,
omniscient, polymorphous, and ubiquitous. On stage he functions as a
master of ceremonies, *raisonneur*, *kurogo*, etc." (182). In sum, the
opposing functions of the protagonic character (Mozart) and the "Joker"
(Salieri) together offer a representation of concrete reality and the
"universalizing abstraction" of it (177).

It is unlikely of course that Shaffer consciously drew upon these
two opposing poetics—that of Aristotle and that of Augusto Boal—in
writing *Amadeus*. However, the implicit existence of a dual poetics
would conform with one of Shaffer's most characteristic inclinations.
The pervasive use of doubles throughout his work (often ascribed to his
twinship with Anthony Shaffer)[8] includes a number of paired opposites,
one passionate and the other repressed: Ted and Bob in *The Private Ear*,
Atahuallpa and Pizarro in *The Royal Hunt of the Sun*, Alan Strang and
Martin Dysart in *Equus*, Lettice and Lotte in *Lettice and Lovage*, and,
certainly, Mozart and Salieri in *Amadeus*. In the latter play, the duality
extends further: the Italians (Salieri and others at the court of Emperor
Joseph II of Austria) are identified with political power and with élitism
in art, preferring operas on heroic themes. The Germans (represented by
the progressively disempowered Mozart) are ordinary people who "smell
of sweat and sausage" and lean toward earthy subjects. In the judgment

of posterity, however, the positions are reversed, for Mozart's work is paradoxically now recognized as "elevated" while Salieri's is pedestrian.

Salieri may have lost the battle artistically, but he still makes no political concession. His Joker-like switch to an identification with ordinary people—when he solicits the complicity of the theater audience and refers to himself as the Patron Saint of Mediocrities (557)—does not mean that he has thrown in his ghostly lot with democracy. Rather, in effect, he is actually asserting a position of dominance by claiming for himself the power of forgiveness. An Eastern Bloc audience, accustomed to reading political meanings into the subtext, will leave the theater mentally shored up to resist the Salieris of the world. Western audiences, whether confused or bemused by the conceit, are more likely to take the implied insult in stride.

It remains then to examine the conundrum of Salieri's last line in the play: "Mediocrities everywhere—now and to come—I absolve you all. Amen!" Various critics have commented on this, asking what empowers Salieri to grant forgiveness to posterity, since he is neither a priest nor a god.[9] If we accept the Joker system, no further explanation is needed. Salieri as the "Joker" can be anything that is dramaturgically or socially useful, and at this point it is useful for him to be a Prospero-like magician, releasing the audience from the spell of the theater and bringing them back to earth with a thudding reminder of everyday failings: it is too easy to turn our backs to the true artists of our time while falling under the sway of facile talent or mere celebrity.

But if we are to analyze the play according to Aristotelian poetics, there must be an organic reason for the apparently strange artistic choice of the play's last line. Dramaturgically, it could be an ironic inversion of a catharsis; as a mediocrity himself, Salieri is incapable of evoking the uplift and transcendence that should be effected by a "tragic hero." Placing the audience on his own level is the best he can do. More satisfying is a combined psychoanalytic and thematic explanation. By claiming for himself the power of forgiveness, Salieri is indulging in a psychological defense mechanism known as identification with the aggressor. According to J. Laplanche and J.-B. Pontalis, "the subject identifies himself with his aggressor. He may do so either by appropriating the aggression itself, or else by physical or moral emulation of the aggressor, or again by adopting particular symbols of power by which the aggressor is designated."[10]  In identifying with God as his aggressor, Salieri also ties the play's ending into the thematic emphasis on fathers.[11] Both Mozart's and Salieri's attitudes toward God were apparently shaped by their relationships with their fathers. As the son of a merchant, Salieri tried to make a deal with God. Mozart served as the instrument first of his father and ultimately with God. When—immediately after declaring his hatred of his father— Mozart is told of his father's death, he grieves: "He watched for me all my life—and I betrayed him."

The parallel is obvious between Mozart's betrayal of his father and Salieri's betrayal of God. Mozart's musical expression of his feelings about his father after Leopold Mozart's death first takes the threatening form of the Ghost Father in *Don Giovanni*, but is later sublimated into the reconciling figure of the High Priest in *The Magic Flute*. This progression is also paralleled in Salieri, who appears menacingly to Mozart as the masked figure in grey and tries to play the role of surrogate father; then his subsequent assumption of the priest's or God's power to absolve sins might be a symbolic reconciliation. Again, such dualities underscore the Shafferian propensity that suggests he may have embraced two different poetic systems, even ones embodied in such opposing figures as the "tragic hero" and the "Joker."

# Notes

1. Paul Lasley and Elizabeth Harryman, "'Amadeus' Raises the Curtain on a New Era in Chinese Theater," *The Christian Science Monitor,* 3 January 1986, p. 1.

2. Peter Shaffer, *The Collected Plays of Peter Shaffer* (New York: Harmony Books, 1982), p. xvi.

3. Aristotle, *Poetics*, translated by Gerald F. Else (Ann Arbor: University of Michigan Press, 1970), p. 32.

4. C. J. Gianakaris, "A Playwright Looks at Mozart: Peter Shaffer's *Amadeus,*" *Comparative Drama,* 15 (Spring 1981): 40–41.

5. Augusto Boal, *Theatre of the Oppressed,* translated by Charles A. and Maria-Odilia Leal McBride (New York: Theatre Communications Group, 1985), p. 40–45.

6. Harold C. Schonberg, "Villain of 'Amadeus' is Hero of Broadway," *New York Times,* 19 December 1980, Sec. 2, p.3.

7. Harold C. Schonberg, "Mozart's World: From London to Broadway," *New York Times,* 14 December 1980, Sec. 2, p. 35.

8. See, for example, Jules Glenn, "Twins in the Theater: A Study of Plays by Peter and Anthony Shaffer," in *Blood Brothers: Siblings as Writers,* ed. Norman Kiell (New York: International Universities Press, Inc., 1983), pp. 277–299.

9. See, for example, Robert Brustein, "The Triumph of Mediocrity," *New Republic,* 17 January 1981, 24; Janet Karsten Larson, "'Amadeus': Shaffer's Hollow Men," *Christian Century,* 98 (May 1981): 579.

10. J. Laplanche and J.-B. Pontalis, *The Language of Psychoanalysis,* translated Donald Nicholson-Smith (New York: W. W. Norton and Co., Inc., 1973), p. 208.

11. For a full treatment of this topic, see William J. Sullivan, "Peter Shaffer's *Amadeus*: The Making and Un-Making of the Fathers," *American Imago,* 45 (Spring 1988): 45–60.

# FAIR PLAY? PETER SHAFFER'S
# TREATMENT OF MOZART IN *AMADEUS*

## C. J. Gianakaris

"I was suddenly frightened. It seemed to me that I had heard a voice of God—and that it issued from a creature whose own voice I had also heard—and it was the voice of an obscene child!" These words, which appear early in Peter Shaffer's drama *Amadeus*, refer to the archetype of all musical prodigies, Wolfgang Amadeus Mozart. The source of this rude judgment in the play is Antonio Salieri (1750–1825) who, romanticized rumor has it, caused Mozart's early death by poison. Shaffer seized on this alleged misdeed to fashion an arresting drama concerning not only Mozart's life and times but the nature of genius, stifled in a humanly flawed world.

Other artists before Shaffer had tapped the same conflict between Mozart and Salieri. Pushkin wrote a play (1830), turned by Rimsky-Korsakov into an opera with the same title, *Mozart and Salieri*, in 1897. These earlier cases caused little stir, though Rimsky-Korsakov's tidy, small-scaled opera received occasional productions. *Amadeus*, however, is another matter.

A theatrical hit from its opening in London in 1979, *Amadeus* also has evoked a vocal band of dissenters. Negative response to the American version has been muted but present as an undercurrent of opinion. Most reservations involve Shaffer's unflattering portrait of Mozart, which some claim unfair and unworthy of such a genius. To judge whether these accusations are justified, we need answers to two related questions: how much tampering has Shaffer done with historic fact, and does he sharpen or blunt our understanding of the Mozart that emerges?

Answers will not be simple, because *Amadeus* brings into account several dimensions of Mozart's life besides his character and career. Mozart's relationship to his father is a focal point of the drama, as are details concerning the musical circles and preferences in Vienna during Mozart's stay in that musical mecca. And of course there is also the issue of Shaffer's figure of Salieri as intriguer and possible poisoner of Mozart. An objective scrutiny of these points should convince us that criticisms of *Amadeus* are groundless, for two reasons. First, Shaffer takes almost no liberties with historical fact about Mozart and his times, except where Salieri the man is concerned. Second, Mozart emerges positively in Shaffer's paradigm, against the backdrop of lesser men's base intrigues.

Most disconcerting to harsh critics of *Amadeus* is the picture of Mozart, in the abstract, that the drama projects. The facts are that, along with undeniable musical brilliance, often charm and verve, also appeared arrogance, coarseness of language, evidence of infidelity and childish behavior in Mozart's character. Such attributes contrast strikingly with the traditional, idealized image. Shaffer has explained that his intent in no way was to demean Mozart. Quite the contrary, he wanted audiences to know Mozart better and more totally—to know a genius of far greater complexity than granted by standard portraits.

At the same time, Shaffer recognized that some could misinterpret the play as implying that Mozart's difficult life and early death somehow were deserved. As a consequence, Mozart's character was slightly toned down for the American version, and the Salieri figure was made more nefarious.

In his preface to the U.S. version of *Amadeus* (Harper and Row, 1981), Shaffer states the case: "One of the faults which I believe existed in the London version was simply that Salieri had too little to do with Mozart's ruin. . . . Now, in this version, he [Salieri] seems to me to stand where he properly belongs—at the wicked center of the action."

Aside from such adjustments to focus the action, Shaffer remained true to his sources. Mozart's scatological bent and frequent puerile actions are verifiable as historical fact. The biggest jolt occurs when audiences first are introduced to the Mozart figure in scene five of the first act. There, Salieri, the play's narrator, inadvertently witnesses the frolicking of Mozart with his intended, Constanze, in the elegant library of a nobleman's palace. To Salieri's amazement, Mozart is first seen on his hands and knees, stalking his finacée around the furniture, mewing like a cat: "I'm going to pounce-bounce! I'm going to scrunch-munch! I'm going to chew-poo my little mouse-wouse!" Moments later, as the lovers tumble about on the library floor, Mozart teases Constanze in jarring, indelicate phrases.

Artistic fabrication on Shaffer's part? Not at all. Epsiodes are cited in several Mozart biographies, such as Henry Raynor's or Fischer and Besch's, recounting animal play-acting, even beyond childhood. More to the point, verbal crudities were part and parcel of Mozart's makeup, as one quickly learns from the composer's letters. Editor Emily Anderson suggests that in addition to the scatological passages to be found there, many more may have been expunged by George Nikolaus von Nissen, Constanze's second husband, known for his prim formality, who "ruthlessly manipulated the letter MSS." In her general introduction to the three volumes of letters, Miss Anderson writes, "Even in Germany an excessive prudishness or possibly a certain unwillingness to admit that the writer, formerly regarded as the Raphael or the Watteau of music, should have been capable of expressing himself with such grossness, has hitherto prevented their publication *in toto*. A study of the whole correspondence, however, shows clearly that it was not only when writing to his 'Bäsle' [Constanze] that Mozart indulged in this particular kind of coarseness, but that on occasion he did so when writing to his mother and to his sister." Evidence of Mozart's linguistic eccentricities has been public since 1938, forty-one years before *Amadeus*.

As for Mozart's lighter word-play, which Shaffer so effectively illustrates in *Amadeus*, again the letters of Mozart serve as genesis. Syllables spliced together into nursery-rhyme patter are found repeatedly in these pages. In letter 236 to his cousin Maria Anna, for instance, he signs off with, "your little old piggy wiggy/Wolfgang Amadé Rosy posy/P.S. Addio, booby looly." And in the same fifth scene from Act I of *Amadeus*, when Mozart teases Constanze with "T-r-a-z-o-m. What's that mean?," the origin once more is found in the letters: 180a, Mozart's postscript to a letter by his father, reveals an early instance of his writing his name in reverse, as he signs off with "Oidda./ Gnagflow Trazom."

Related to Mozart's childlike behavior is his relationship to his father, Leopold. The reservoir of correspondence among Mozart family members makes clear the extremely difficult life Mozart and Constanze led in terms of financial solvency. Late in life, the composer was forced to write countless letters to his Masonic brothers and other friends, asking or pleading for loans of money. For a combination of reasons, Mozart never had sufficient funds to be relieved of onerous teaching and composing chores.

Playwright Shaffer has commented that Leopold Mozart had so strictly conditioned his son as a child prodigy that Wolfgang was never capable of managing his life and finances. *Amadeus* offers explicit passages to that effect, as well. Near the play's end, Constanze lashes out concerning Mozart's father, claiming their penury was "all his fault . . . I hated him. . . . And he hated *me*." Mozart's sister, Nannerl, has been quoted as saying that "Outside of music he was, and remained nearly always, a child. This was the chief trait of his character on its shady side. He always needed a father, mother or other guardian."

Though Shaffer did not write a part for Leopold in *Amadeus*, the elder Mozart nonetheless exists as a strong presence, affecting the hero's attitudes and actions at every turn. Is Shaffer accurate in creating the image of a nagging, guilt-projecting father? Biographical materials again show that he is. Turning once more to the letters, we find ambivalence on Mozart's part regarding his father. Anderson believes such facts are essential to an understanding of the younger man's genius, adding that despite the bond of music "which was never broken," the relationship between father and son finally gave way when young Mozart attempted to take charge of his own life. His growing bond with the Weber family provided an alternative to the reliance on his father that had begun at age six, when Wolfgang was carted around Europe to perform.

Shaffer alludes a great deal to the love/hate connection between Leopold and Wolfgang, and in the revised American version of the play he goes even further, integrating Salieri, the beseeching Masked Figure, the Commendatore from *Don Giovanni* and Sarastro from *Die Zauberflöte* into a single essence, that of Leopold. Shaffer's preface to the American edition pinpoints the changes: "This new, more active Salieri offers himself as a substitute father when Leopold Mozart dies. . . . And it [a new scene] enables me to transform the huge accusing silhouette of Leopold-as-Commendatore, seen on the backdrop, into the forgiving silhouette of Leopold-as-Sarastro, his hands extended to the world in a vast embrace of love."

Has Shaffer really succeeded in attaining dramatic excellence without doing violence to the facts of Mozart's life and career? Each spectator will make his own judgment about *Amadeus* as drama. As for its accuracy as history, we might welcome further consideration of Salieri and the nature of Viennese musical circles and tastes of the time. Based on the materials examined here, we can affirm that Shaffer *has* followed factual sources to a remarkable degree. The result is an authentic, candid portrait of Mozart that opens up his more human qualities. Shaffer's depiction also confirms the aptness of the name Amadeus (Beloved of God) for Mozart, for it is *his* music, not Salieri's, that became a staple in our heritage.

# GAME-PLAYING IN FOUR PLAYS BY PETER SHAFFER: *SHRIVINGS, EQUUS, LETTICE AND LOVAGE,* AND *YONADAB*

## Dennis A. Klein

From his earliest detective novels to his most recent plays, Peter Shaffer's works are characterized and united by the technique of game-playing among the characters. In the detective novels of the 1950s, Shaffer's sleuths trick the criminals into revealing their guilt, much as Dr. Dysart in *Equus* has to deceive Alan Strang into disclosing the details of his crime. Most of Shaffer's plays in fact are constructed on games. In *Five Finger Exercise* (1958), Clive plays a poseur game with his mother in order to retain her love and stay free of her wrath. In *White Lies* (1967) and *The White Liars* (1968), Sophie, Frank, and Tom all play identity games with each other, much as Brindsley does with Clea and Carol in *Black Comedy* (1965). (And all the while, Shaffer plays a game of reversal of light and darkness with the spectator.) Ted plays a game of false friendship with Bob in *The Private Ear* (1962) which serves to foreshadow much more destructive deceptions by Antonio Salieri in *Amadeus* and by the title character in *Yonadab*. Julian Cristoforou plays a silence game with Belinda and an empty-threat-game with Sidley in *The Public Eye* (1962). The most serious game—one of life and death—takes place between Pizarro and Atahuallpa in *The Royal Hunt of the Sun* (1964).[1] Game-playing is in full bloom in *Shrivings* (1974),[2] *Equus* (1973), *Lettice and Lovage* (1987), and *Yonadab* (1985).[3]

One of the clearest instances of game-playing appears in *Shrivings*. The historical Shrivings was a house of retreat in the Middle

Ages; likewise, in Shaffer's drama, Shrivings is a house of peace, headed by Gideon Petrie, philosopher and president of the World League of Peace. Also living in Shrivings are Lois Neal—Gideon's twenty-five-year-old American secretary—and David Askelon—nineteen-year-old son of Mark Askelon, a poet and former student of Gideon who now has become a stranger to his own son. The play begins on a Friday evening before a weekend peace vigil has been scheduled to include Gideon and his followers. Harmony in the the house is destroyed from the moment Mark sets foot in it. He ridicules the whole peace movement, knowing that to the others in the house it is a very serious cause; and he criticizes Lois, a vegetarian, for imposing her moral standards on the rest of the inhabitants of the house. He has everybody at everybody else's throat before the end of the play. Like *The Royal Hunt of the Sun, Shrivings* essentially is a battle of wills between two men—here, Gideon the peace advocate and Askelon the godless cynic.

The pivotal point in the plot concerns The Apple Game. Mark bets Gideon that in just one weekend he can upset the House of Peace so completely that Gideon will ask him to leave. That event would constitute a victory of hate over love, and Gideon would have to acknowledge it as such. If Mark loses, he would again become Gideon's disciple and give up his corrosive beliefs: "That the Gospel According to Saint Gideon is a lie. That we as men cannot alter for the better any particular that matters. That we are totally and forever unimprovable" (156).[4]

To prove his point, Mark insists that they all play The Apple Game, which is based on the real-life experiment in which subjects were instructed to administer what they believed was electric shock to innocent victims. For his version of the game, Mark lines up a series of apples which he identifies as representing everything along the continuum from mild shock to The Death Apple. Then he has his son David tie him to a chair, and insists upon the right to say anything he wishes. He contends that he will be able to make someone push The Death Apple. Gideon and Lois try pressing the "mild" apples, and they see that Mark responds. To make one of them push The Death Apple and win his wager, Mark pulls out all the stops: he begins to reveal secrets and to speculate about Lois's and Gideon's sexuality. Lois lives with Gideon, he says, because she knows that she is safe there since there can be no sex with him. Nor did Gideon's wife leave her husband just because he gave up sex but because she could no longer stand the hypocrisy of living with him. Mark's attack on Gideon is merciless when he says to Lois,"Don't you know the only sex Gideon ever really enjoyed was with boys? Slim brown boys with sloping shoulders? . . . The world saw only a Great Renunciation on the grandest philosophic grounds: but not so Enid [Gideon's wife]. All she saw was a self-accusing pederast, pretending to be Gandhi!" (177).

Mark's campaign of attack most affects David who had become close to Gideon. David first gets uneasy, then angry, and finally outraged. He picks up The Death Apple signifying life or death for his father and smashes it over and over. Mark Askelon "dies" and by the rules of the game clearly wins the contest. Lois is angered with David for rising to the bait, and she wants Gideon to tell Mark to leave Shrivings. But Gideon cannot do it; rather he wants to smother Mark with understanding and acceptance.

Confrontation and confession mark the outcome of the game. Lois and David want to know how much of what Mark said was true, and Gideon feels compelled to respond:

> When I was young, I had, as they say, sex on the brain. I meant by that, that even when I worked on equations, or read Political Science, the impulse of my attention was somehow sexual. Sex was everywhere. A girl's hair bobbing down the street. The sudden fur of a boy's neck. The twitching lope of a red setter dog. In flowers, even— the smell of cow-parsley in the field of poppies would almost make me faint. To say I was bi-sexual would have been a ludicrous understatement. I was tri-sexual. Quadri. Quinti. Sexi-sexual, you might say! (182)

Gideon insists, however, that his wife Enid left him for the reason he always had claimed, namely, his abandonment of further sex in his life: "The decision was too rigorous for her" (183).

Before Mark Askelon is finished, he thoroughly destroys the harmony once characteristic of Shrivings: he gets David to break the fast by eating meat, thereby violating Gideon's announced vigil; he makes Lois miss the peace rally altogether; he casts doubt on whether he in fact is David's true father; he seduces Lois; and he accuses his son David and his pot-smoking generation of not being able to "get it up to

save [their] stoned lives!" (197)—thus transforming Gideon into a
blatant hypocrite and accusing his son of being an "unmale."

Mark, an alcoholic trying to escape from his own guilts,
confesses that he killed his crippled wife by forcing her to watch while
he made love with another woman. Furthermore, the hypocrisy that
Askelon identifies at Shrivings is not the central problem for him. He
cannot bear the contentment of any of the residents of the House of
Peace, not when he is so joyless and passionless: "Inside me, from my
first day on earth, was a cancer. An incapacity for Immediate Life"
(189). By the end of the drama, Shrivings can never be the same again.
Gideon loses his respect for Lois; she calls Shrivings "nowhere"; and
David, now a lost soul, turns on Gideon, his former idol and mentor:
"Theories and hopes and vigils and fasts! *And nothing! Lovely nothing!*
. . . FUCK OFF!" (200–201).

Game-playing holds a central position in Shaffer's hit drama
*Equus* as well. In that work there are three crucial games that take place
in the course of Alan Strang's psychotherapy: The Answer-in-Turns
Game, The Blink Game, and The Placebo Game. *Equus*, concerned with
a psychiatrist and one of his patients, is based on an actual case history
of a boy who blinded a stable full of horses with a metal pick. Shaffer
builds his dramatic work on that core event. In the play, after Hesther
Salomon, a magistrate, gets court permission to send Alan for
treatment rather than to prison for blinding the horses, she comes to Dr.
Martin Dysart, whom she considers the only person capable of helping
young Strang. It is immediately clear to Dysart that no traditional
method of question-and-answer analysis will work with the disturbed
but wily boy who refuses to respond to Dysart's questions with
anything but jingles from television commercials. Thus Dysart and
Alan must rely on games.

Alan seemingly wants Dysart's help, but the analysis cannot be
painful—it must take the form of a game. In fact, the lad himself
suggests the first game: he will answer Dysart's questions if the doctor
will answer his—each in turn, one question each. Alan urges this game
for two reasons: first, it will make the analysis easier on him, and,
second, he will get to know Dysart the man better—a man becoming
important in Alan's life since the horse-blinding deeds. Throughout the
scene, Dysart is unable to elicit information from Alan. When he tries
to discover why the boy cries out "Ek" in his sleep, Alan begins
singing one of his jingles. To the question regarding Alan's first

memory of horses, Alan claims that he cannot remember. All the lad manages to discover about Dysart meanwhile is that he is married and that he dreams about carving up children (a fact which gets a smile out of Alan). Only at the final moment of the scene when Dysart refuses to talk further to Alan does the boy offer any genuine information, mumbling "On a beach" (37).

The next scene clarifies where Alan had his initial experience with a horse. What began as a game, at Alan's suggestion, ends up giving Dysart insights into the youth's problem with horses and his parents. Alan's parents are a religious mother and an atheistic father. The father blames the lad's problems on his wife for reading him "kinky" stories from the Bible about how an innocent man was whipped and made to drag a cross up a mountain. Alan for some time had a picture of Jesus in his room, described by his mother as "a little extreme. The Christ was loaded down with chains, and the centurions were really laying on the stripes" (44). When his father insisted that the picture be removed, Alan replaced it with one of a horse with huge, bulging eyes. One night, Mr. Strang explains to Dysart, he caught Alan in front of the picture with a piece of string in his mouth (as a bit) and a coat hanger with which he was beating himself, all the while chanting parodies of biblical genealogy. The psychiatrist then realizes the boy had created a religious ritual with a horse-god at its center.

From Mr. Dalton, owner of the stables where Alan had worked, Dysart learns about Jill, the young girl who got Alan his job with the horses he eventually harmed. Try as he might, Dysart at first is unable to get Alan to talk about Jill; he succeeds only in enraging the lad. The doctor has enough of the The Answer-in-Turns Game but is willing to undertake one final round if it will bring out information concerning Jill. Although Dysart still gains little knowledge about the girl, Alan expresses his suspicions that Dysart and his wife no longer indulge in sex. In his monologue at the end of the scene, the physician admits that the subject of his wife is his "area of maximum vulnerability" (59) and that the troubled boy had assessed the situation with total accuracy.

Next, Dysart asks Alan to play The Blink Game, which he tells the boy will make him feel better. Alan is to fix his eyes on an object and close them in response to the tap of a pen, thereby to be placed under hypnosis. In this scene, Alan shows how strong a Jesus/horse identification he has built up in his mind. He also reveals his secret midnight horseback rides. Those rides had begun as religious rituals and ended up as sexual acts.[5]

Through monologues to the audience and conversations with Hesther, Dysart discloses key details of his own life: his marriage is passionless and his greatest fascination lies in classical Greek civilization. Moreover, the psychiatrist admits an envy of Alan who *lives* his passions and fascinations rather than merely reading about them in books, as does the doctor. But to find out more about Alan, Dysart must rely on games. Ultimately, to bring the therapy to its climax, he plays The Placebo Game with Alan. He senses that his patient is ready to unburden himself (Alan as much as told him so in a note slipped under the doctor's office door), and Dysart believes this final game should work. In preparing the lad for the last game, Dysart never lies but allows Alan to draw his own conclusions:

| | |
|---|---|
| ALAN: | You got another trick, then? |
| DYSART: | Yes. |
| ALAN: | A truth drug? |
| DYSART: | If you like. |
| ALAN: | What's it do? |
| DYSART: | Make it easier for you to talk. |
| ALAN: | Like you can't help yourself? |
| DYSART: | That's right. Like you have to speak the truth at all costs. And all of it. (84) |

Painfully, Alan finally tells about Jill. She arranged for his job at the stables and one night asked him on a date to a skin flick. He was transfixed by the sight in the film of a woman taking a shower—his first look at a naked woman. Suddenly, Alan's father entered the movie house and spotted the boy; but equally significant to Alan was his catching his father there. While confused and upset at discovering his father at such a movie, Alan agrees to Jill's suggestion that she and Alan steal away to the stables for a tryst. Alan eventually was convinced because he was attracted by Jill's eyes and by the promise of a first sexual experience with a girl.

But Alan's first love affair proved to be a disaster. Each time they kissed, Alan "heard" the hooves of the horses in the adjoining stable and he pulled away. Finally, Jill undressed, as did Alan. Once on the floor with the girl, Alan was plagued by the noise of his horse-god

Equus in the next stable, and his attempt at sex was ruined. Under hyponosis, Alan insists to Dysart that he and Jill indeed made love: "I put it in her. . . All the way. I shoved it. I put it in her all the way" (100). The doctor realizes that Alan is lying, however, and ultimately gets him to admit that Equus intruded each time the boy tried to become intimate with Jill. When he touched her, he felt horse-hide. The possessed Alan—his face contorted—reenacted the episode when he ordered Jill out of the stable. Then, left alone and naked, he picked up a metal pick, crying out to the horse called Nugget, "Equus . . . Noble Equus . . . Faithful and True . . . Godslave . . . Thou—God—Seest—NOTHING!" (103). And he stabbed out the horse's eyes. In Alan's narrated reenactment two more horse-gods appear, and then three more: *"Their eyes flare—their nostrils flare—their mouths flare"* (103). Before he had finished, Alan stabbed out the eyes of six horses. Exhausted and traumatized by his abreacted ordeal, Alan wanted to be found and punished. Once the psychological wound has been lanced, however, Dysart can cure the lad of his obsession with horses and return him to the "normal" world. But there will be a price, as the doctor explains: "Hopefully he'll feel nothing at his fork but Approved Flesh. *I doubt, however, with much passion!* . . . Passion, you see, can be destroyed by a doctor. It cannot be created" (106).

There is even a higher price to be paid for Alan's "recovery," one assessed to the psychiatrist himself. Alan may be freed from his psychological distress, but Dysart sees no hope for curing what has become his own personal anguish. Dysart ends the drama, lamenting his own new predicament: "There is now, in my mouth, this sharp chain. And it never comes out" (106).

Mark Askelon's Apple Game is vicious, and it leaves psychological scars on the residents of the House of Peace; Dysart's games have therapeutic results but may leave Alan without passion. Three games played in Shaffer's *Lettice and Lovage* range from harmless to dangerous to destructive. Charlotte (Lotte) Schoen leaves her London Office of the Preservation Trust to track down complaints at Fustian House in Wiltshire concerning tour guide Lettice Douffet. By tagging along on one of Lettice's narrated tours, Lotte quickly determines that her guide indeed is taking liberties with historical fact concerning the Tudor mansion—a building Lettice declares to be the dullest house in England. Like Sophie found in the three versions of *White Liars*, Lettice believes that "Fantasy floods in where fact leaves a vacuum."[6] The day after discovering Lettice's historical infelicities, Lotte fires her. Paradoxically, however, Lotte is so impressed by Lettice's "spunk" during the firing interview that a friendship between the two eventually evolves. What started as mutual hostility and dislike ends up in a relationship in which the two spinsters learn that deep down they are in fact soulmates.

The two protagonists engage in three games during the course of the comedy. The first takes place in Lettice's flat in Earl's Court several weeks after her dismissal from the Trust. During the intervening weeks, Lotte hears of a position on a sightseeing boat on the Thames for which Lettice might be well suited. Consequently, Lotte visits Lettice to learn if she is interested in the position. That visit changes both their lives. As Lotte admits in the final moments of the play, "My life began again when I first walked down those stairs [to Lettice's basement flat]" (94).

It is on the occasion of Lotte's first visit to Lettice that their initial game-playing commences with The Interview Game. Under the influence of a strong dose of lovage (a potent drink made of mead, vodka, sugar, and parsley), Lotte is willing to participate in a diversion in which Lettice pretends to be interviewing Miss Schoen for a job. The first objective for the player is to learn the interviewee's first name as well as other information about her. It is a reversal of roles in which Lotte, always the interviewer in her professional life, becomes at Lettice's suggestion the interviewee. Lotte reluctantly agrees. It is similar in form and content to Alan's game in *Equus* for asking Dysart questions about his private life.

During the initial game in *Lettice and Lovage*, Lettice learns that Lotte's German-born father owned the Perseus Press which specialized in art books. Mr. Schoen suffered a financial reversal after his wife ran off with another man. Lotte meanwhile never completed her course in architecture following the break-up of her romance with a fellow student. Like Miss Furnival in *Black Comedy* Lotte finds that drink loosens her tongue. Thus, as with Alan who craves a truth serum, the lovage allows Lotte to speak freely.

The libations technique also exposes something about Lettice's background—for instance, that she enjoys playing games. She reveals too her discomfort with modern, mechanical society. One of her affectations (like Louise Harrington's in *Five Finger Exercise*) is sprinkling her speech with French words. Lettice's pleasures include the theater, while British history is another passion. Lettice's ancestry—like Louise Harrington's—is partly French. Lotte and Walter Langer (from *Five Finger Exercise*) share a German background in common.

The interviewing pattern is long-standing in Shaffer's plays. Louise Harrington employs it to find out as much as possible about Walter's past. Sophie (in all three versions of *Lies* and *Liars*) interviews Tom and Frank before consenting to engage in their Identity Game. Dysart uses it extensively in his exploration of Alan's psychosis, as we have seen. Lettice and Lotte meanwhile, perhaps without even intending to, reveal to each other how similar their values and ideals are, thereby providing the basis for a bond of trust and friendship. It starts with a fact as simple as Lotte's father having published books that brought Lettice so much pleasure, and affinities continue with both women's ardent interest in British history. The plot starts to take shape when Lotte mentions she had studied architecture, a profession much admired by Lettice for its artistic and cultural ramifications.

Interestingly, the relationship between the two women in this work parallels that of masculine characters in several of Shaffer's other plays—and not just Alan Strang's association with Dysart. The bonding that takes place between them points back to scenes involving Clive and Walter in *Five Finger Exercise*. It also approximates the intimacy that develops between Pizarro and Atahuallpa in *The Royal Hunt of the Sun* before the Spanish general is compelled to have the Incan Emperor executed.[7] The bond deepens when the two protagonists decide (at Lotte's suggestion) to become "a little fanatic" about what is happening to their city. It is not until the end of the play, however, that the playwright resumes that theme and brings it to a satisfying conclusion.

The first act of *Lettice and Lovage* would lead a spectator or reader to think no common ground existed between the two heroines. Lotte is Dysart to Lettice's Alan. Once again it is the voice of reason versus the spirit of passion, the defender of fact and order against the lover of fantasy and imagination. That dichotomy breaks down in the play as it does in the archetypal pattern between Don Quixote who speaks for idealism and Sancho Panza who only sees physical reality. Lettice can fan the spark of passion that previously could only smolder deep within Lotte.

Both women agree that London is in a pathetic state because it is bereft of citizens displaying spunk. They will not themselves join the ranks of the "Mere People" and the "Ghosts," however. Lettice's reference to "Mere People" is something like Sophie's reference to "Rubbish people" in *White Lies* and her reference to the world's Takers, "emotional peasants" in *The White Liars*. Lettice and Lotte will be Givers, the emotional aristocrats of the world, and they are going to earn that position by destroying what is ugly and leaving only what is lovely. Lotte articulates the case:

> That was the true Age of Destruction—the late fifties and sixties. You realize the British destroyed London ultimately, not the Germans. There would be gangs of workmen all over the place, bashing down our heritage, whole terraces of Georgian buildings crashing to the ground. I still see those great balls of iron swinging against elegant facades—street after street! All those fanlights shattering—enchanting little doorways—perfectly proportioned windows, bash, bash, bash!—and no one stopping it. It was exactly like being hit oneself. (51)

Lotte will do with Lettice what she did not have courage to do with her former boyfriend, Jim: destroy what is too ugly to exist. (Shaffer's revision of the play alters the manner that the heroines rebel, but their opposition to institutional ugliness remains the same.) To that extent Lettice is replacing Jim in Lotte's life. Lettice sees herself and Lotte as "A natural team. An expert in architecture and an expert in weaponry. It's a formidable combination" (93).

The event that almost lands Lettice in jail for attempted murder also started out as a game—The Execution Game. To celebrate the spunk shown by courageous heroes over the centuries, Lettice and Lovage each Friday evening act out the trials and executions of famous historical figures—women as well as men, foreigners as well as Britons. Usually Lotte would portray the executioner, but on one occasion she wanted to switch roles with Lettice, much as Alan liked to switch roles with Dysart. On 31 January, the two chose to enact the execution of Charles I to commemorate the anniversary of his beheading in 1649. On this occasion Lotte insisted on playing the king. In a technique of abreaction paralleling that Dysart uses with Alan in the final scene of *Equus*, Lettice and Lotte relive for Mr. Bardolph—Lettice's court-appointed solicitor—the exact events from the night of the alleged crime. Lettice narrates how Lotte as king rose from her "throne," standing "with all the passion of the Stuarts surging through her" and "actually *became* the King, walking to his martyrdom!" (79)— all the while reenacting Charles's journey across St. James's Park to the balcony at Whitehall. The two women then proceed to act out the actions leading to the accidental violence. While Lotte as king knelt down before the executioner's block, Lettice as henchman stood above her, axe in hand. Suddenly Lettice's cat bounded into the room to startle Lettice, causing the axe to drop on her companion's head, resulting in serious injury. During the reenactment for Bardolph, it becomes clear how infectious Lettice's spirit is as well as her passion for theater. Not only has she won over the formerly severe Lotte to her play-acting manner, but she even convinces the staid Bardolph to take part by becoming the make-believe drummer playing at Charles's execution.

At first Lettice is only minimally concerned about her pending trial for the alleged physical assault of Lotte, because she is certain Lotte will come to her defense. Yet Lettice also expresses some anxiety lest Lotte elect to betray her trust. The themes of trust and betrayal abound in Shaffer's theater as far back as the relationship between Young Martin and Pizarro in *The Royal Hunt of the Sun* and as recently as Yonadab and Amnon, with Mozart and Salieri along the way. Lotte seems sure that the entire problem can be straightened out with little fuss. Her testimony will prove critical to get Lettice off. However, Lotte experiences grave reservations about testifying publicly regarding the women's play-acting sessions, as that fact surely will destroy Lotte's responsible career with the Trust. Eventually, Lotte sees that Lettice can only be exonerated by the full disclosure of their game-playing, and she agrees to explain all in court; but Lotte briefly regrets her free-spirited association with Lettice and declares an end to their friendship.

But another change of heart in Lotte reunites the London spinsters, and they begin to make plans for yet one more "game," what might be termed The Demolition Game. The object of this final game device is to target the ten ugliest buildings in London. In the original version of the play, the two intend to destroy the errant structures by bombing them, thereby to rid London of some of its modern visual blight; but Shaffer amended the extremeness of their plans for his revised text so that they plan guided tours of the ugly buildings, instead, and not their actual destruction. When they have implemented

their tour designs, Lotte will have exonerated herself from having
betrayed Jim earlier by failing to follow through against encroaching
ugliness in the city. Lotte's transformation is complete when she
begins employing the phrases Lettice used previously in Lotte's office
during Lettice's exit interview. Now Lotte advocates "Enlargement for
. . . shrunken souls Enlivenment for . . . dying spirits; Enlightenment
for . . . dim prosaic eyes" (95).

   While Lettice and Lotte are serious about revolting against the
modern, unsightly architecture of London, the prospect of such an
undertaking also is a game to them. They enjoy topping each other in
listing buildings to be their "targets"; Lettice enjoys the idea of having
Elizabethan weapons attacking contemporary structures (in the early
version of the play); and there is an irresistibility in carrying out their
E. N. D.—Eyesore Negation Detachment—and to embarrass the
materialistic civic leaders of London. Who would suspect two innocent
spinsters of such spunky deeds? Lettice is ready to act not just because
she would see "All the monstrosities we detest—vanishing one by
one!," but also because "the police would be powerless to stop it! . . .
They'd never catch up—they couldn't begin to guess the motive. No
one attacks buildings just because they're ugly!" (94—first version of
the comedy).

   The final game appeals to Lotte because it gets her out of her
office, away from the "Non-Doer's Desk" and makes her involved in
measurable action. It will keep her from sitting among "ghosts" and
becoming one herself: "Ghosts! They're the worst! That's what we
must never become ourselves—you and I," she tells Lettice (47).
"Ghosts" in one form or another appear in all four plays treated here.
Dysart feels no more than the shadow of a man, which also is true of
Yonadab. Mark Askelon also feels like a ghost separated from the world
around him. In that respect he is a forerunner of Lettice who senses
herself alienated from modern society. She explains to Lotte: "You're
wrong when you say there's nothing ghostly about me. That's what *I
am*. Every day more . . . It grows every day . . . It's like a mesh
keeping me out—all new things, every day more. *Your* things.
Computers. Screens. Bleeps and buttons . . . The whole world I
understand isn't there! . . . *Everything's* gone for me! . . . *I'm* the
foreigner . . ." (90–91). Similarly, anywhere Mark Askelon goes, he
too feels like a foreigner, an outsider with no place to call his own:
"We are not Place People, David or I. My father was not called

Askelon, but Ashkenazy. Israel Ashkenazy, of the ghetto face. He bequeathed me no home on earth: only envy of home in others" (152). Like Pizarro, Alan, and possibly Dysart, Lotte claims to be an idolator.

The image of eyes, so prominent in *Equus* as well as in *Yonadab*, is also important in *Lettice and Lovage*. Just as the all-powerful eyes of Equus "watched" Alan and cursed him, so too Lotte's perceptive eyes are her curse. She wishes she had not inherited her father's eyes. "I wish I was blind, like everyone else," she complains (50). If she were blind like the horses that were Alan's victims, her eyes would not be assaulted by the ugliness they now see around her. The image of eyes is the bridge between *Lettice and Lovage* and *Yonadab*.

The Voyeur Game in *Yonadab* is the key not only to that play, but possibly to all four in this study. *Yonadab* is the least known of Shaffer's works since it has not yet had a professional production in the United States—only in London where it opened late in 1985. *Yonadab* also repeats the structure, character types, and themes on which Shaffer's fame rests. As in *The Royal Hunt of the Sun, Equus*, and *Amadeus*, a character narrates the plot and in the course reveals his own problems. *The Royal Hunt* is rooted in the history of the Spanish conquest of Peru; *Amadeus* uses the historical characters of Wolfgang Amadeus Mozart and Antonio Salieri; and *Equus* derives from a real-life crime. *Yonadab* has the most time-honored source of all—the Bible. Specifically, the source is II Samuel, where Yonadab (or Jonadab), a nephew of King David, advises Amnon, the King's eldest son, to commit incest with his half-sister Tamar, the king's only daughter and fruit of the union with Bathsheba the Princess of Israel.[8] Yonadab proposes to supply the motivation of deceit on the part of all of the characters in the drama that the prophet Samuel omitted from his writing.

In a set reminiscent of that of *Equus*, stylized and with some of the actors sitting around the outer stage, Yonadab—in early middle age—reveals the play's focus to be on deceit and ruin, a theme similar to that of *The Royal Hunt of the Sun*. Yonadab's problem, like that of Pizarro and Dysart, is his inability to believe in conventional divinity. Like Salieri and Mark Askelon, he feels empty, devoid of passion, and separated from the rest of the humanity. He bears resemblance to both Pizarro and Alan Strang who need a form of worship that does not include God. Pizarro hoped to be able to replace Catholicism with the Incan worship of the sun; Alan replaced Jesus with Equus. Yonadab tries to replace Jewish law and its practices during the time of King David with something gentle and personal. As Yonadab explains to the audience, "Yonadab the Creep. That actually is what you become when you bow to One God because you're terrified of stones—but long in your heart for another altogether, who has no use for stones" (I, i). Like Salieri, Yonadab suffers from his own invisibility; he too is a "ghost." The punishment for his crime is that he lives forever in limbo. As such, he resembles Salieri who must spend forever mentally reliving his destruction of Mozart.

Yonadab's crime, which he thought would solve all his difficulties, was that of being a voyeur—or at least trying to be so— while manipulating the whole royal family in his scheme. Yonadab has long yearned for a Kingdom of Perpetual Peace ruled by a king and queen deeply in love, a place with no ferocious Judge and no commandments of Thou Shalt Not. And he longs for an understanding of the power of prayer: "I know Gods cannot walk on earth:—let it be! I know lovers cannot infect Kingdoms:—let it be! Let there be an end to this world of blood-soaked worship—and to my unchanging world! Set this manipulating man at last in way of *meaning*! . . . Let me believe!" There is considerable irony in this speech. It is a prayer to make him believe in prayer, addressed ostensibly to the God in Whom he does not believe. It may be less in God that he does not believe than in himself.

Amnon—whose body is better developed than his mind—makes the same mistake that destroys Young Martin and Mozart: he trusts the man he thinks is acting in his best interests, here Yonadab. Amnon has two emotions that are bound up in each other as the play begins, lust and guilt, much like Alan's circumstances. His sexual desires for Tamar have passed the point of denial, but he also knows "Thou shalt not uncover the nakedness of thy sister. Nor thy half-sister" (I, iii), and that the penalty for doing so is stoning. Yonadab makes it his job to turn sin into obligation: Thou shalt, Thou must. Like Mark who complains about the "Rabbis of Repression," Yonadab refers sarcastically to the "Priests [who] keep you woefully ignorant, you know. For your own good, no doubt."

For a variety of reasons, Yonadab takes it upon himself to mastermind a plan that will enable Amnon to have sex with Tamar. In part he is seeking revenge against King David who never took seriously the idea that Yonadab could be a suitable candidate for marriage to his daughter; in part he is getting back at Tamar who hardly deigns to look at him; and in part he is currying favor with the legitimate heir to the throne. There also is the prospect of watching the "Bull" (David's nickname for his sexually powerful son) in bed with the beautiful princess. Like Dysart and Mark Askelon, Yonadab can experience passion only vicariously by watching it in others. Like Salieri, Yonadab is at war with God, the only Being Who can stop his evil plan. His own explanation is chilling: "To make it happen—calamity! Ruin to the great who sneer! to the House of David for whom I didn't exist! Ruin even to the *God* of David!—why not? Let Him defend Himself! Prove that He exists, *finally*! Let Him stop me if He is there. Yaveh the Prohibitor" (I, iii). Yonadab's view of the God of Thou Shalt Not calls to mind the image of the Deity as it exists in Alan's mind—under the influence of his mother—and of Equus the Judge who punishes him.

The Voyeur Game is one incident in the play, but The Deception Game permeates the drama. Yonadab informs the audience in his opening monologue that his is "a tale of total deceit" and that every character is both deceiver and deceived. And so it is. Yonadab deceives both Amnon and later Absalom into believing that they can fulfill divine destiny by having sex with Tamar. Amnon deceived his father and sister by claiming that he needs Tamar to nurse him back to health. Absalom deceives King David by claiming that he wants Amnon killed for his crime in order to avenge his sister's honor, when in fact he undoubtedly wants his chief rival for the throne out of the way. David deceives the people by refusing to enforce the law that is his responsibility. Tamar deceives Absalom into believing that she was led to his house by some magical spirit; and she deceives everyone by planning Amnon's murder after overhearing a conversation between her brother and Yonadab.

Yonadab tells Amnon that in congress with his sister he will become immortal. Yonadab thus stimulates Amnon's curiosity and vanity. Yonadab explains that "The Kings of Egypt are Gods to this day. . . . in the Kingdom of the Nile they believe if a man is truly royal he shares in divinity. . . . in Egypt they say that if you are really a Prince immortality is your *birthright*. It's inside you, just waiting to be born" (I, iii). The prospect is now irresistible to Amnon: not only will he satisfy his lust; he will become a god and fulfill his destiny.

Yonadab clearly enjoys manipulating David's royal family—one that holds him in low esteem, especially as he brings about the violation of Tamar. He concocts a story that brings Tamar to Amnon's bedchamber, and he then arranges to leave the two alone to attain divinity. Almost alone, that is. In return for the favor of delivering Tamar to Amnon's bed, the Prince must let Yonadab watch. But Amnon does not agree, and Yonadab must hide behind a plant as Amnon takes his sister to bed. In addition, Yonadab can see no more than silhouettes on the curtain that Amnon draws. Just as Pizarro believes that he will see Atahuallpa experience immediate resurrection after execution, and just as Martin Dysart believes that Alan Strang is approaching sexual divinity on his rides with Equus—so Yonadab believes that he will see Amnon and Tamar transformed into gods on the spot. Of course, it does not happen that way. Amnon so much wants to believe Yonadab's lie that when he fails to become a god, that sexual experience for him becomes the basest of acts. Amnon terms it "just another fuck," and orders his "whore," "witch" sister—whom he holds responsible for his disappointment—to be thrown out of his house into the streets.

In the closing moments of the drama, Yonadab reveals the motivations that drive and control him. Like Pizarro, Mark, Dysart, and Salieri before him, Yonadab wants meaning, substance, and faith in his life: "I saw all their transports, this royal family—their lusts for transcendence:—and I saw nothing. Always the curtain was between us. . . . Always between me and men that curtain" (II, xiv). That curtain serves as a metaphor for those who cannot experience the passion of life, only alienation. Moreover, the curtain becomes a unifying device to bind Yonadab to his predecessors—Shaffer's other protagonists who are victims of their own existential angst. Yonadab sees lack of faith as his great curse, which he explains in terms reminiscent of Shaffer's other heroes: "Always on me the curse of that man [King David]! Watch forever unmoved. To see the gestures of faith in others, telling me no more than the gestures of their flesh!" If Yonadab's curse so expressed in these words recalls Pizarro and Mark Askelon, it is Dysart's last lines that are echoed in Yonadab's final pronouncement: "Yonadab hangs in Yonadab's world, attached to the Tree of Unattachment. Who will cut me down?"

Several minor unifying threads run through the plays considered here. One of them is history, most often British history. Shrivings was a House of Retreat in medieval England. Lettice's "crime" against Lotte takes place on the anniversary of the execution of King Charles I. Alan

Strang receives his information about history from his mother; his favorite King of England is John "Because he put out the eyes of that smarty little—" (28). King John was known to have some of his prisoners blinded; in the case of Arthur, the King was advised to have him both blinded and castrated. There also is the subject of "unnatural" acts. Alan's erotic desire is for horses; Amnon commits incest; and as a youth Gideon Petrie was excited by almost anything that moved. *Lettice and Lovage* may be included in this category for a reference that Lettice makes to Marie Antionette, who she says was accused of having relations with her own son.

If there is thematic unity in the techniques of games in these dramas, there also is circular, geographical unity in Shaffer's plays. His first script for television in 1955 was "The Salt Land," in which refugees from Europe sail to find the Promised Land in the modern State of Israel. In *Yonadab* one distraught resident of ancient Israel convinces a simple-minded prince that through a forbidden sexual act he can bring about the Kingdom of Perpetual Peace—an objective Shaffer's characters seem incapable of attaining.

# Notes

1. There is detailed treatment of these plays in my book *Peter Shaffer* (Boston: Twayne Pub., 1979).

2. The original version, produced in London in 1970, was called *The Battle of Shrivings*. Shaffer rewrote the play and published it as *Shrivings* in 1974.

3. *Yonadab* opened at the National Theatre in London on 4 December 1985, with direction by Peter Hall and set design by John Bury; Alan Bates originated the title role. Shaffer rewrote the play for New York, but it has not yet been produced. The manuscript of the revised version is the basis of this study. Since it remains unpublished as this essay is being written, I refer in the text of my essay to act and scene rather than to page numbers.

4. Peter Shaffer, *Equus* [and] *Shrivings* (New York: Atheneum, 1974). All page references to these two works are from this edition and appear in the text of the study within parentheses.

5. For discussions on the relationship between sex and religion in the play, see, among other studies, Hélène L. Baldwin, "*Equus*: Theater of Cruelty or Theater of Sensationalism?," *West Virginia University Philological Papers*, 25 (1978): 123; Klein's *Peter Shaffer*, pp. 121–122; and John Weightman, "Christ as Man and Horse," *Encounter*, 44, No. 3 (March 1975): 46.

6. All citations are from the first version: Peter Shaffer, *Lettice and Lovage* (London: André Deutsch, 1988).

7. For a psychiatrist's treatment of "doubles," see the following articles by Jules Glenn: "Anthony and Peter Shaffer's Plays: The Influence of Twinship in Creativity," *American Imago* 31 (1974): 270–292; "Twins in Disguise: A Psychoanalytic Essay on *Sleuth* and *The Royal Hunt of the Sun*," *Psychoanalytic Quarterly*, 43, No. 2 (1974): 228–302; and "Twins in Disguise. II. Content, Form and Style in Plays by Anthony and Peter Shaffer," *The International Review of Psycho-Analysis*, 1, No. 3 (1974): 373–381.

8. More so even than the Book of Samuel, Shaffer's source of inspiration for the play was Dan Jacobson's novel *The Rape of Tamar* (New York: Macmillan, 1970).

# "WHERE ALL THE LADDERS START": THE AUTOBIOGRAPHICAL IMPULSE IN SHAFFER'S RECENT WORK

## Michael Hinden

I was seated next to Peter Shaffer on the dais of a large ballroom in a New York hotel, the occasion being a panel on the playwright's work presented at the 1983 convention of the Modern Language Association. Mr. Shaffer was responding graciously to questions from the audience prompted by the papers just delivered. I was rather nervous: here was the celebrated artist in person poised to tell the world, were he so inclined, that what had just been said about him was folderol. Shaffer was the soul of courtesy, but I had reason to feel uncomfortable, for in my paper I had briefly touched on biographical matters about which he might have been sensitive.[1] All went well until an energetic person rose in the back of the hall and demanded to know what the dramatist thought about biographical criticism. Shaffer's response has lingered in my mind, and it has shaped the reading that I am about to present of his two most recent plays, *Yonadab* and *Lettice and Lovage*.

Many dramatists who have distinctive visions tend to repeat patterns in their plays—we think no less of their work for that. We keep bumping into patients in Strindberg, doctors in Chekhov, social misfits in Williams, guilty fathers in Ibsen, and guilty sons in O'Neill—to cite but a few examples. Shaffer's plays are populated with recognizable figures too. From the beginning, his work has been preoccupied with characters in competition, usually two male rivals, jousting by means of challenges, games, or deceit.[2] In analyzing affinities between *Shrivings*, *The Royal Hunt of the Sun*, and *Equus*,

Joan F. Dean early on described "a recurrent character type" in Shaffer's oeuvre: a middle-aged man in a crisis of faith who seeks illumination from contact with some primitive force.[3] *Amadeus* continued the pattern, as was noted by several critics who dealt primarily with Shaffer's religious themes.[4] Shaffer's typical protagonist now could be described more completely as one tormented by doubts about religion and career in conjunction with sexual or artistic failure. This sufferer is drawn to an exotic younger man—be he genius or misfit or both—who seems favored by the gods with those qualities the protagonist most envies.

A bonding process then links these rivals; the pattern can be traced in its development through the relationships of Clive and Walter in *Five Finger Exercise*, Bob and Ted in *The Private Ear*, Frank and Tom in *White Liars*, Charles and Julian in *The Public Eye*, Pizarro and Atahuallpa in *The Royal Hunt of the Sun*, Mark and Gideon in *Shrivings*, Dysart and Alan in *Equus*, and Salieri and Mozart in *Amadeus*. In some instances the characters behave almost as doubles (Dysart and Alan, for example). As the sequence progresses, Shaffer devotes greater attention to the religious yearnings of his central characters and in so doing creates a platform for disquisition on larger philosophical issues. In Shaffer's best known work, the figures compete with God, and the design of the earlier rivalries is transposed to a more sonorous key. Several of Shaffer's recent protagonists (notably Salieri) follow the rebellious Satanic model, declaring evil to be their goal and all-out war on the cosmos.

Such was the outline of my argument in that initial talk, which expressed admiration for Shaffer's dialogue and then went on to describe the critical response to his work. In that connection I could not fail to mention a controversial series of articles by the psychoanalyst Jules Glenn, who has written extensively on the similarities between Shaffer's plays and those of his fraternal twin Anthony (the author of *Sleuth*). According to Dr. Glenn, the rivals who appear in both brothers' plays are invariably "twins in disguise" competing for their parents' undivided attention.[5] The displacement of anger from earthly father to Heavenly Father seems but a natural step to Glenn.[6] Furthermore, he argues, twins often entertain the fantasy of being half a person and dream of connection with their sibling, who can be both a rival and a double—an observation that might help to account for Shaffer's recurrent character type. Ultimately, Glenn argues, the twin relationship is fraught with anxiety: "the special organization of love and hate found in many twins includes intense drives that require discharge and forbidden elements."[7]

Glenn's theory of course is open to all the objections commonly lodged against psychoanalytic criticism: it scants literary values, blurs variety, is dogmatic, reductive, and dismissive of all but unconscious content in the work of art.[8] It also is difficult to put out of mind once you have heard it, and as I neared the end of my paper at that convention of the Modern Language Association, I could not forbear noting a curious parallel. Is it merely coincidence, I wondered aloud, that the protagonists of *The Royal Hunt of the Sun, Equus,* and *Amadeus* are all jealous of rivals whose names begin with the letter "A"? Atahuallpa, Alan, Amadeus: "A" as in Anthony, Peter Shaffer's twin.

"Mr. Shaffer," piped the voice from the back of the hall at the conference, "would you care to respond to critics who keep looking for hidden meanings in your plays? And in particular [*pause; exasperated glance in my direction*], would you care to comment on some of the views we just heard in the last paper?" I tried to sink under the table and succeeded, I believe, in occupying the smallest possible space consistent with my undeniable presence on the dais. But Shaffer responded with his customary kindness and humor. "Well," he began, "it is always interesting to learn what people may be thinking about your plays. Critics are forever pointing out aspects of your work that you never dreamed were there. I suppose that is their prerogative. I am not going to comment on specific theories, but you can be sure of one thing: as soon as a writer is told that he is repeating himself, that will be the end of it!"

I returned from the conference and announced to my class on modern drama: "there will be no more characters whose names begin with 'A' in Peter Shaffer's plays." I was glad to be off the hook and had resolved never again to trouble Shaffer's serenity with the theories of Dr. Glenn. But Shaffer since has written *Yonadab*, a biblical epic in which "fraternal rivalries" and "unnatural desires"[9] are bluntly expressed in terms of murder and incest, and in which rival half-brothers, both envied by the narrator, are named Amnon and Absalom. The pattern in *Yonadab* is so insistent, and the play so revealing, that I must return to that earlier discussion of possible biographical elements in the works of Peter Shaffer.

It may be of significance that Shaffer had been thinking of writing *Yonadab* since 1970, when he first was inspired by Dan Jacobson's novel *The Rape of Tamar* (New York: Macmillan, 1970). According to Shaffer's own account, other work kept intervening and the project was continually deferred: "Always, however, through fifteen years the desire remained with me."[10] The play was completed and produced in 1985 and revised in 1987. But its delayed genesis suggests that the unwritten *Yonadab* served as an "Ur" text in Shaffer's imagination during those years when he worked on *Shrivings, Equus,* and *Amadeus.* In mining the contents of *Yonadab,* he refined and blended its ore elsewhere. Ironically, now that the parent play has arrived, it seems overly indebted to its offspring.

Based on an episode in the Book of Samuel (the original source of Jacobson's novel), *Yonadab* replicates in bold outline the motifs of Shaffer's major dramas.[11] Like Martin in *The Royal Hunt of the Sun,* who narrates for us the dance of death between Pizarro and Atahuallpa, Yonadab watches the growing rivalry at King David's court between his cousins Amnon and Absalom. Bereft of passion and faith (like Dysart and Pizarro), Yonadab attaches himself first to one brother, then to the other, inflaming their incestuous desires for their sister. Yonadab's motives at first are worldly, to gratify his voyeuristic lust and to increase his power over the brothers, who are heirs to the throne. But like Salieri, he also intends to provoke some response from a silent God. Yonadab falls victim to his own manipulation when he actually begins to believe the fantasy that he encourages in the brothers, namely that the incestuous union of royal siblings can change them into demi-gods (a notion derived from Egyptian mythology). If that can happen, then Yonadab might dislodge the Israelites' tyrannical deity, "Yaveh the Savage, with no female consort to soften Him" (*Yonadab* 1987, I, i, 89).

The stage is set for one of Shaffer's most disturbing yet spectacular pantomimes. The hidden Yonadab watches and waits for the epiphanic climax as Amnon brutally rapes his half-sister Tamar. The shadows of their writhing bodies are cast on the bed curtains "like the letters of some grotesque language formed long, long before writing." Yonadab continues: "There on the fall of a Jerusalem drape I saw, writ enormous—like the parody of our Hebrew consonants—the archaic alphabet of the Book of Lust" (*Yonadab* 1987, I. vii. 127). Yet no new revelation follows, no new tablet inscribed with some truth strong enough to cancel the Mosaic commandments. In bitter disappointment, Amnon reports that "it was just another fuck" (*Yonadab* 1987, I, vii, 128), and Yonadab's hope to witness the birth of divinity is frustrated.

Because Absalom has sworn an oath never to kill his brother, Amnon goes unpunished at first, while Tamar secretly plots her own revenge. Her deception is the mainspring of the second act. By feigning belief in the royal incest myth, she tantalizes Absalom with the promise of eternal bliss if he will forswear his oath and dispatch Amnon. Not only is Absalom taken in, but so is Yonadab, and the second act doubles back on the first. Yonadab becomes convinced that his dream was prophetic, after all:

> Absalom and Tamar—riding together upon huge golden horses—jouncing and gleeful up the high road to Jerusalem. On their heads sat golden crowns. On their shoulders golden cloaks. And from their palms streamed golden light. (*Yonadab* 1987, II. vi. 151)

So he dares to hope that Tamar and Absalom, incestuously united, will usher in the new dispensation. Amnon's rape, he decides, was merely a prelude; Absalom remains a virgin at twenty-two, long-haired, beautiful, shining, desirable—and he is Tamar's full (not half) brother: the genuine article. Yonadab is captivated. He enters Absalom's service and sets about manipulating events. Once again wrought to the pitch of excitement, he plans to watch as one sibling kills the other and sexually possesses yet a third.

It does not—cannot—happen. Amnon's murder is spectacular enough, a ritual spearing accompanied by mime and music (a moment on stage carefully arranged in counterpoint to Tamar's "tearing" in Act I), but no coupling follows, nor any new dispensation. Instead of ending with a golden couple riding in on glorious steeds, the play leaves us with the groteque image of Amnon's corpse slung over a mule, his head under its hole, with dung falling in his mouth. (This may be meant as a parodic image of Christ's entry into Jerusalem; it is clearly an image of defilement and, incidentally, a striking inversion of Alan's triumphant pose on the back of Equus.) Absalom's rebellion fails, his death follows, and the old order in the kingdom is shored up for the time being. Tamar's cry is for justice, not love, and certainly not ecstacy.

*Yonadab* seems baroque, with its air of the forbidden and its seething passions, violence, and dark shadows; but in its doublings, flourishes, and gilded circumlocutions, the play invites comparison with the rococo. If its momentum seems to falter in the second act, it is probably because the premise of the play has been thoroughly realized in the first. Why *two* episodes of incest—one consummated, one a misleading stratagem? There is no obvious answer, except to say that the structure of *Yonadab* is compulsively repetitious. At peak moments the play has the quality of an irresistible dream. During these episodes, forbidden contents are disclosed, and then even the play's repetitive rhythm seems appropriate. The difficulty with *Yonadab* is that we cannot involve ourselves completely with the play's narrator, who harangues and titillates us without ever losing *himself* in the action. Some instinct in Shaffer appears to be working to keep his protagonist at a distance from events. Similarly, the audience is compelled to watch everything over Yonadab's shoulder, to watch the Watcher.

Shaffer's plays always have been visually stunning, but *Yonadab* is unique in that its voyeurism is foregrounded, incorporated into the plot. The organization of the stage frames the scene to be enacted with a chorus of anonymous "Helpers" who ring what the directions describe as the "Outer Stage" so as to focus our gaze on the "Inner Stage." The arrangement is somewhat similar to the set for *Equus*. Again, as in *Equus*, eye imagery is featured prominently,[12] along with stabbing imagery. The conjunction of images conveys a sense of shame and guilt at being seen in a forbidden place. There is a strong emphasis on dreaming in the play; the characters envision their own punishments in dreams.[13] Amnon dreams of being led through the streets by his siblings with a rope tied around his genitals (earlier in the play he had begged Yonadab to castrate him). Yonadab, who is called "The Man of Eyes," dreams that Absalom is pointing a sword at him while dogs snap at his thighs. Absalom, in turn, dreams of watching helplessly while Amnon rapes his sister, and Yonadab actually does watch this transgression. Yet his voyeuristic desire is frustrated at the last moment when Amnon draws the curtains: only the shadows of the act are visible to Yonadab and to the audience. Similarly, Amnon's assassination is hidden from our view by a huge woollen carpet, which the Helpers have spread on the Inner Stage. Significantly, Shaffer has commented that the play's dominant image for him remains one of curtains "hiding what must not be looked on."[14]

So we arrived at what can be shown only through shadows and dumbshow in this play of veils and curtains, those ultimate acts forbidden to siblings: incest and fratricide.

Fratricide appears elsewhere in Shaffer's work,[15] but in broaching the incest taboo, he has taken a risk. Murder is common enough on stage, but few modern dramatists have dealt openly with incest; the topic is too disquieting. In order to analyze Shaffer's use of the incest motif, we might consider the writings of Janine Chasseguet-Smirgel, who treats incest and the violation of other sexual taboos as refusals to recognize difference. Incest, she points out, refuses to recognize generational difference; it violates the distinction between parents and children. As with parent-child incest, sibling incest violates the distinction between blood and non-blood relations. Homosexuality subverts gender difference (Shaffer treats that subject in *White Liars* [16]), whereas bestiality ignores the difference between species (an issue that is raised by *Equus*). Evidently, the undoing of difference has a powerful appeal for Shaffer's characters. With respect to *Yonadab*, it is especially instructive to consider the following passage from Chasseguet-Smirgel:

> The pleasure connected with transgression is sustained by the fantasy that—in breaking down the barriers which separate man from woman, child from adult, mother from son, daughter from father, brother from sister . . . it has destroyed reality, thereby creating a new one . . . the universe of the *sacrilege*.[17]

The ultimate aim of the pervert, she concludes, is "to take the Father-Creator's place in order to make a new universe from chaos and mixture,"[18] a description that fits Yonadab perfectly.

Amnon's incestuous desire is the means employed by Yonadab to serve his greater lust, which is "to bring things down" (*Yonadab* 1987, I, iii, 98). As he lingers behind the curtains during the rape scene, it seems to him that the terrible tearing is not only of linen but of all that gives life order. Yonadab's quarrel with difference is philosophical and pervasive. He mocks the Jewish dietary laws, which proscribe the mixing of certain foods; he cannot distinguish between King David's faceless sons; and he denies any distinction between Israel's enemies, lumping them together as the "Ites" whom "you cannot tell apart because we smote them so completely" (*Yonadab*

1987, I. i. 88). Language frustrates him because he finds intolerable the difference between signs and things.[19] Most significantly, he chafes under the rigid sexual prohibitions of the Law with its endless distinctions between clean and unclean: "None of you shall approach anyone near of kin to him to uncover nakedness. I am the LORD" (Leviticus 18:6).

There are seventeen specific variations of this injunction in Leviticus (i.e., "You shall not uncover the nakedness of your sister, the daughter of your father or the daughter of your mother, whether born at home or born abroad"). Yonadab wages his campaign against the Lord on a platform of annihilating all the rules. His ultimate desire is to overthrow God the Father and to usher in the era of the divine incestuous couple, thereby replacing monotheism and its sexual restrictions with polytheism and the polymorphous perverse.[20]

In the end, his quest is defeated. "For the sake of our Law— which alone distinguishes us from beasts," Absalom demands that Amnon be put to death (*Yonadab* 1987, II, i, 134), and so he is eventually. Similarly, Tamar enforces Absalom's banishment on the legalistic gound that he has violated an oath. However, in her eyes his real crime, like Amnon's, has been his incestuous desire for her. While raging at Absalom, Tamar reaffirms monotheism: "Did you think I would believe such evil? You and I—Gods? . . . GODS? . . . There is only One God in Heaven!" (*Yonadab* 1987, II, xiv, 176). She also reaffirms the authority of her father, whose rule had been jeopardized by her rebellious brothers. Fleeing the King's wrath, Absalom is caught in a tree by his tresses and is hanged. It is Tamar who pronounced his epitaph in one of the play's most revealing lines: "There was no difference between the brothers. Not in the end. No difference, bull or beauty" (*Yonadab* 1987, II, xiv, 177).

The subtext crackles with Old Testament thunder: the penalty for the brothers' erasing of difference must be death. In the final speech of the play, Yonadab, who has staged this drama, mourns his separateness, which is the obverse of the brothers' incestuous desire and yet another kind of death: "Yonadab hangs in Yonadab's world, attached to the Tree of Unattachment. Who will cut me down?" (*Yonadab* 1987, II. xiv. 182). Like Salieri, he is a ghost, floating in some perpetual limbo, waiting to snare an audience, condemned for eternity to be *unattached*.

Twinship's Complaint? Yes, but much more. If Claude Lévi-Strauss is correct, the incest taboo and the proscription against homicide are bound together at the root of our civilization and culture: They define our notions of self. Consider the Oedipus myth. According to Lévi-Strauss, it is comprised of two dialectical patterns, the *underrating* of blood relationships (the slaying of kin) and the *overrating* of blood relationships (incest). Can there be any deeper anxiety than that of misconstruing the boundaries of one's identity? The Oedipus myth for Lévi-Strauss further "provides a kind of logical tool which relates the original problem—born from one or born from two?—to the derivative problem—born from different or born from same?"[21] With Shaffer, the ancient question is posed like this: Was *I* born one or two, different or same? What are the parameters of self, and what does it mean to be separate? No doubt the defining moment in Shaffer's plays occurs when Alan Strang mounts Equus and rides into the night calling:

> Bear me away!
> Make us One Person!
> [*He rides EQUUS frantically.*]
> One person! One person! One person! One person![22]

There may be an autobiographical element in this speech, but Alan's cry is as old as civilization.

There can be no personality without boundaries, but there exists within all of us an urge to dissolve those boundaries from time so as to experience the seductive (but also threatening) bliss of undifferentiated oneness. Such is the warrant of mysticism. Freud, however, explained the urge as a remnant of infancy and associated the desire with the death-wish.[23] Whatever may be its explanation, this drive motivates Shaffer's dramaturgy, and it returns us to the very origins of theater. Nietzsche, we may recall, grounded his explanation of the birth of tragedy in the quest for undifferentiated oneness. His inspired guess was that, from the beginning, drama was rooted in the joy and terror felt by spectators who identified with actors imitating the great egotistical personalities of Greek myth, personalities that were projected through "Apollonian masks," which in the course of the drama were shattered to disclose "Dionysian wisdom."

Nietzsche's theories suggest a special kind of magic:

> Under the charm of the Dionysian . . . all the rigid,
> hostile barriers that necessity, caprice, or 'impudent

> convention' have fixed between man and man are
> broken. . . . Each one feels himself not only united,
> reconciled, and fused with his neighbor, but as one with
> him, as if the veil of *maya* had been torn aside and were
> now merely fluttering in tatters before the mysterious
> primordial unity.[24]

Shaffer's stagecraft aspires to approximate that magic Nietzsche describes. Employing masks, mime, ritual, dance, and music, Shaffer's theater attempts to disclose the mysterious ambivalence of the self when presented with the opportunity of transcendence. Perhaps he comes closest to achieving that aim in *Equus*. It is *Yonadab*, however, that remains Shaffer's ultimate play of veils, a work whose symbolism, according to the playwright's testimony, resides in "the many different kinds of curtain suspended before the eyes of my protagonist."[25]

What is it, then, that requires muffling in *Yonadab*, that remains unspeakable? Is it desire for sexual congress so dreadful that it cannot be admitted? Or is it desire for a psychological closeness so threatening to self-possession that its only adequate metaphors are incest and fratricide? Dr. Glenn's hypothesis does have explanatory power in this connection, for in the case of sibling rivalry between twins, the most uncompromising alternatives for the twin would be to annihilate his double or to merge with him, even though that would mean annihilating the self. Both impulses are forbidden, giving rise to self-torment and guilt. "Blessed art Thou, King of the universe, who hast given us bread from the earth!" King David tells his sons, "And blessed be he who eats it in peace with his brothers" (*Yonadab* 1987, I, i, 90). In their division, Absalom and Amnon, like Shaffer's other major characters, cannot rejoice. They envy God for being almighty and alone.

Unveiling this perspective renders part of the hidden content of *Yonadab* more accessible. But the issues involved extend beyond the sibling rivalry contest. Fratricide and incest as metaphors mirror the psyche's dilemma whenever it is made miserable by desire and seeks to restore its well being. At such moments its choices are to deny or to possess. To deny annihilates the object of desire, which has posed a threat to equanimity, but it also involves shedding an aspect of the self that has come into being as a result of desire. To possess attains the object of desire but does so by surrendering some of the difference between self and object. That can occur by means of conquest, but conquest soon tires of possession. To attain the object of overwhelming desires means desiring the self to be overwhelmed in turn as it attains its goal: for that emotion, the incest metaphor has its resonance. Shaffer's work, I suspect, appeals to such subterranean knowledge in us, even when as in *Yonadab*, its surface current appear to be running elsewhere.

After the spectacular trilogy of *Equus, Amadeus,* and *Yonadab* (or tetralogy if we include *The Royal Hunt of the Sun*), Shaffer penned *Lettice and Lovage*, which might be described as a comic *scherzo* —or, to continue the analogy with the Greek Festival of Dionysis—as a satyr play, a work replicating the themes and situations of his tragic sequence in jocular form. In many respects, as C. J. Gianakaris rightly observes, *Lettice and Lovage* signals a break from Shaffer's theatrical practice of the last twenty years to return to the comic mode that he exploited with dexterity earlier in his career. The setting is contemporary, the style is realistic, the tone witty, the subject matter seemingly far removed from the metaphysical issues that are associated with Shaffer's recent work.[26] And yet familiar elements appear in recombinant form. As Gianakaris suggests, the Dionysian/Apollonian conflict takes a lighter turn here in the tension between the play's two leading characters, Lettice (the "Dionysian free spirit") and Lotte (the "Apollonian authority figure").[27] But the pattern remains, all the same.

In the opening act we are introduced to Lettice Douffet, who is the tour guide at what must be the dullest of England's great houses. In retelling the history of Fustian House, Lettice likes to enliven fact with the embroidery of romance and adventure. "Fantasy," she remarks, "floods in where fact leaves a vacuum."[28] Lotte Schoen, who represents the Preservation Trust, has joined the tour on this day to eavesdrop on Lettice, having received complaints about her "bizarre inaccuracies" (I, i, 14). The two women confront each other in the next scene, which takes place in Lotte's London office. Lotte upholds truth over fiction, and history over theatricality; she has no choice but to dismiss Lettice, who sweeps out of her office with a grand flourish. Throughout this act the two certainly do seem cast as opposites. Lettice sports theatrical dress; Lotte is aggressively plain. Lettice is naturally exuberant; Lotte is severe. Lettice despises machinery; Lotte despises the theater and is taking a computer course. But what is striking here in relation to Shaffer's other work is that the *difference* between these "opposites" dissolves in the next act.

Ten weeks have passed when Lotte presents herself at Lettice's basement flat, ostensibly to help her former employee find a new position. Over drinks (a special brew containing an herb called "lovage"—whence the play's title), the two grow more familiar, and Lotte admits that what prompted the visit was her attraction to Lettice's spunky spirit. As they converse, it appears that the two women have much more in common. Both are middle-aged and alone in life; both were raised by single parents to whom they were devoted (Lotte's mother abandoned her father, Lettice's father abandoned her mother); both have been influenced by exposure to foreign cultures (Lotte's father was German; Lettice was raised in France); both prize the arts (Lettice inherits her love of theater from her mother, who was an actress; Lotte inherits her aesthetic sense from her father, who published art books); both favor disguises; both admire the heroic figures of the past (persons who had displayed "spunk"); and both despise contemporary architecture.

Indeed, in some respects they are more like doubles than opposites. As in the case of *Yonadab* (Amnon/Absalom), the repetition of their initials (Lettice/Lotte) reinforces the impression of doubling. Later, as the two begin to act out historical dramas, they literally exchange roles, playing victim and executioner by turns. Lotte adopts Lettice's flair for the dramatic gesture. At the end of Act I, Lettice flamboyantly changes her costume in front of Lotte; at the end of Act II, Lotte mimics the action, removing her wig in front of Lettice as a gesture of intimacy. Lettice responds in courtly fashion, laying her cloak ceremoniously at Lotte's feet in the manner of Sir Walter Raleigh assisting Queen Elizabeth.

Soon the two lonely women are on close terms: they spend their weekends engaged in mutual fantasy, acting out the trials and executions of a few selected monumental spirits—Mary Queen of Scots, Sir Walter Raleigh, King Charles I. The scene enactments are Lettice's idea. While growing up, she served as the stage manager for her mother's acting company which toured the Dordogne playing Shakespeare in French. She has imbibed her mother's passion for history plays, and, feeling as she does persecuted, she identifies with those famous royal victims of the headsman's axe. In this macabre theater for two with its limited repertoire, the evening always ends with an execution.

One of these scenes, as recounted by Lettice, is of particular note, given the obsession of *Yonadab*. Lettice relishes the part of Marie Antoinette, who stood in the dock defying her accusers when they charged her with incest (III.73). This peculiar detail suggests that in Shaffer's imagination *Lettice and Lovage* may bear some of the traces of a conflict that is given more overt expression in *Yonadab*. In the comedy, however, the negation of difference between the principals is accomplished by means of laughter rather than violation, as the two join forces to overcome the barriers that separate them.

Violence nevertheless is present as an undercurrent in the play through grisly references to mutilations (the chopping off of hands in *Titus Andronicus*) and sundry decapitations. (One has the impression that the stabbing/castration imagery of *Yonadab* is carried over into *Lettice and Lovage* by some unconscious momentum.) As the curtain rises in Act III, we see that the front door to Lettice's flat has been smashed, and we discover that Lettice has been charged in a criminal assault against Lotte. She must reconstruct events for her solicitor, and as she does so, we learn that during one of their dramas, Lotte, playing Charles I, was wounded in the head when Lettice, playing the Cromwellian executioner, accidentally nicked her with an axe. Coincidentally, a passing constable witnessed the scene through a window and broke down the door in alarm.

The significance of this incident is central to the theme, for according to Lettice, the beheading of Charles by the Puritans meant the symbolic castration of England:

> All the color! The age of color! The painted churches!
> The painted statues! The painted languages! they're all
> about to go forever!—at one stroke of an axe! In their
> place will come gray! The great English gray! The gray
> of Cromwell's clothes! The gray of Prose and Puritanism,
> falling on us like a blight forever! (III, 86)

The enactment, though, is a comic reversal of the historical moment: Lotte, the supposed Puritan, is *almost* beheaded by Lettice, the representative of theatricality and other anti-Puritan values.

If the dialectic of *Yonadab* is framed in terms of sexual pleasure *versus* repression, then the dialectic of *Lettice and Lovage* is framed in terms of aesthetic pleasure *versus* Puritanism, here defined as hatred of all that is beautiful or voluptuous. But Lotte, it turns out, is not Lettice's nemesis. "I am not a Christian," Lotte asserts, "and the only good I perceive is in beauty" (II, 47). Her statement suggests how close the two women actually are in sensibility. Moreover, at the close of the play, Lettice and Lotte pledge to join forces against the Puritan spirit, which (if one grants Shaffer's premise) has transmigrated from politics to the soul of contemporary British architecture. Like Yonadab, Lettice and Lotte desire to bring everything down, and there is even some talk about blowing up buildings in the earlier version of the play.

There are additional parallels with *Yonadab*. As in the previous play, patriarchy is rebuffed as a repressive force, aligned with the authoritarian mode associated with a Puritan political order. Lotte, the more straight-laced of the two women, was raised by a stern father who taught her to view the world through "the Communal Eye" (II, 51). Like other fathers who appear in Shaffer's plays, he seems to have been a domineering figure. In *Amadeus*, Leopold infantilizes Mozart by forcing him into the role of a child prodigy, a burden from which his personality never recovers. In *Equus*, Alan Strang's father blocks his desires at every turn, pulling him off horses and out of porno-movie houses. In *Yonadab*, King David exercises absolute power and control over his sons, stirring them to rebellion. However, in *Lettice and Lovage* a positive role model is provided in the figure of Lettice's high-spirited mother, who encouraged her daughter to play (in every sense of the word). "Enlarge! Enliven! Enlighten!" was her motto (II, 50), and Shaffer appears to celebrate through the memory of Alice Evans Douffet the benefits of a non-authoritarian, matriarchal dispensation.

Toward the end of the play a dark moment threatens to separate the protagonists. Bardolph, the solicitor, describes the embarrassment awaiting the women when they are brought to court: this dose of reality prompts Lotte momentarily to revert to her former persona, and she proposes breaking off the relationship with Lettice. Lettice feels spurned (her word), and in the most heartfelt speech of the play confesses to Lotte her sense of abandonment. The speech is effective; Lotte returns. What is most unusual about this speech, though, is its means of delivery. Lotte already has gone out the door when Lettice begins speaking, so Lettice appeals to her through the intercom telephone that can be heard just outside the front door of the apartment where Lotte has exited. Lotte is stopped in her tracks (we can see her legs through the bay window of Lettice's basement flat). By any account, this seems an unusual stage device, and it suggests an uncanny parallel to *Yonadab*. Once again Shaffer has interposed a screening device at the crucial moment of a relationship. The comic tone here, of course, is very different from that of *Yonadab*, yet echoes of the earlier play are present: her rivalry and attraction are masked by mock combat, and here too intimacy is veiled.

What is veiled at the conclusion of *Lettice and Lovage* is an attachment between two women that diverges from the heterosexual norm.[29] While there is no sexual contact between the pair, nor even a hint of physical desire, Lettice and Lotte unite at the end with a nod to the ancient marriage convention of comedy. The evening ends with the clinking of a toast, as *"the two ladies swirl their goblets in unison"* (III, 99). In contrast to the imagery of impotence that marks the close of *Yonadab*, the celebratory mood at the close of *Lettice and Lovage* is positively orgasmic. Music *"swells,"* souls *"enlarge,"* liquor *"cascades,"* and on behalf of her partner, Lettice offers the audience a *"brimming good-bye"* (III, 98–99). In view of the pair's parallel parentage, tastes, and proclivities, we may say that Lettice and Lotte constitute a comic version of the divine incestuous couple of which Yonadab dreamed.

From the beginning, Shaffer's art has been consecrated to exploring a powerful root experience that may seem frightening or joyous depending on mood, but which is always there. The playwright cannot trifle with this experience, and that is why nothing that Shaffer writes ever seems trifling, even his comedies; yet he can express emotion in an astonishing variety of forms. To seek out some of the patterns underlying this variety is by no means to diminish the fertility of Shaffer's imagination. On the contrary, it is worth looking for a figure in the carpet only when that carpet is brilliantly colored and enticing.

In "The Circus Animals' Desertion," W. B. Yeats reflected on the mysterious relationship between art and the unconscious. The poet, he acknowledged, is always engaged in disguising from himself the bodily origins of his work. Looking back on his career, Yeats was bemused: "Players and painted stage took all my love,/ And not those things that they were emblems of." Now, in old age, he was determined to interrogate himself and to respond without equivocation:

> Those masterful images because complete
> Grew in pure mind, but out of what began?

> A mound of refuse or the sweepings of a street,
> Old kettles, old bottles, and broken can,
> Old iron, old bones, old rags, that raving slut
> Who keeps the till. Now that my ladder's gone,
> I must lie down where all the ladders start,
> In the foul rag and bone shop of the heart.[30]

There is a bodily muse raving in Shaffer too. The playwright may or may not choose to follow Yeats' example by exposing her to public scrutiny, but his players and his painted stage—his masterful images—are on display and invite interpretation. Where does Shaffer's ladder start? Is Dr. Glenn's hypothesis correct in tracing Shaffer's inspiration to the biographical circumstances of twinship? Such a guess remains speculative, and as a cautionary note, perhaps we ought to recall Martin Dysart's compaint that the psychoanalytic field is a fabricator of false causalities. Still, those who are interested in Shaffer's career cannot entirely dismiss Glenn's theories. I suggest that the critic be encouraged to place *his* ladder where he will—against the top row of the balcony or stowed beneath the stage. From every angle in Shaffer's theater, the view is fascinating.

# Notes

1. The paper subsequently was published: "Trying to Like Shaffer," *Comparative Drama,* 19 (1985): 14–29.

2. Dennis Klein, *Peter Shaffer* (Boston: G. K. Hall, 1979), p. 144.

3. Joan F. Dean, "Peter Shaffer's Recurrent Character Type," *Modern Drama,* 21 (1978): 297–305.

4. C. J. Gianakaris, "A Playwright Looks at Mozart: Peter Shaffer's *Amadeus,*" *Comparative Drama,* 15 (1981): 37–53; Michael Hinden, "When Playwrights Talk to God: Peter Shaffer and the Legacy of O'Neill," *Comparative Drama* 16 (1982): 49–63; Gene A. Plunka, *Peter Shaffer: Roles, Rites, and Rituals in the Theater* (Rutherford, N.J.: Fairleigh Dickinson Univ. Press, 1988), pp. 177–196; Larry Bouchard, *Tragic Method and Tragic Theology: Evil in Contemporary Drama and Religious*

*Thought* (University Park, Pa.: The Pennsylvania State Univ. Press, 1989), pp. 176–215.

5. Jules Glenn, "Anthony and Peter Shaffer's Plays: The Influence of Twinship on Creativity," *American Imago*, 31 (1974): 270–292; Glenn, "Twins in Disguise: A Psychoanalytic Essay on *Sleuth* and *The Royal Hunt of the Sun*," *The Psychoanalytic Quarterly*, 43 (1974): 288–302; Glenn, "Twins in Disguise. II: Content, Form, and Style in Plays by Anthony and Peter Shaffer," *Blood Brothers: Siblings as Writers*, ed. Norman Kiell (New York: International Univ. Press, 1983), 271–291.

6. Glenn, "Twins in the Theater," p. 283.

7. Ibid., pp. 281–282. Glenn mentions homosexuality and sadomasochistic elements.

8. Shaffer is conversant with Glenn's theory but rejects it. According to Gene Plunka, who raised the matter in an interview with the playwright, Shaffer characterized Glenn's work as arrogant, distorted, and parasitic. See Plunka, *Peter Shaffer*, pp. 31, 205 (notes 13, 14).

9. This characterization of the play is given by Yonadab himself in the opening monologue of Shaffer's unpublished 1985 script, though the line was cut in the revised version of 1987. I am grateful to Professor C. J. Gianakaris for providing me with a copy of the 1985 typescript of the play, from which I quote. The quotations will be identified parenthetically by date, citing act and scene numbers alone for the unpublished version. Shaffer's revised version of *Yonadab* now is available in *Lettice and Lovage and Yonadab* (London: Penguin Books, 1989). Quotations from the 1987 version also will be noted parenthetically but as 1987, followed by act, scene, and page numbers from this published edition. *Yonadab*, incidentally, premiered in London in 1985, directed by Peter Hall at the National Theatre. It opened to mixed reviews.

10. Shaffer's program note to the National Theatre production, reproduced in Virginia Cooke and Malcolm Page, *File on Shaffer* (London: Methuen, 1987), pp. 73–74.

11. Dennis Klein discusses many of the parallels in "*Yonadab* : Peter Shaffer's Earlier Dramas Revisited in the Court of King David," *Comparative Drama*, 22 (1988): 68–78.

12. In *Yonadab*, Amnon regards Tamar's eyes as prophetic signs that they were meant to cohabit and achieve immortality.

13. For a general discussion of how dreams function in Shaffer's plays, see Dennis Klein, "A Note on the Use of Dreams in Peter Shaffer's Major Plays," *Journal of Evolutionary Psychology*, 9 (1989): 25–31.

14. A comment in Shaffer's program note to the National Theatre production of *Yonadab*, reproduced in Cook and Page, *File on Shaffer*, p. 74.

15. In Shaffer's early television play "The Salt Land," one brother kills another. In *The Royal Hunt of the Sun*, Pizarro is fascinated to learn that Atahuallpa murdered his brother in order to rule without competition. In the play Pizarro and Atahuallpa become like brothers before the Inca is killed.

16. Homosexuality as an expression of defiance is the subject of a speech by Yonadab that has been cut from the revised published version: "I never wanted men sexually—although the yapping prohibition of the Priests might just have led me to lie with some fellow a little prettier, just for the defiance of it" (*Yonadab* 1985, I, iii). Several commentators have suggested that homoerotic attraction may be a theme in other plays by Shaffer. See, for example, John Simon, "Hippodrama at the Psychodrome," *Hudson Review*, 28 (1975): 97–106; Jeffrey Berman, "*Equus* : After Such Little Forgiveness, What Knowledge?" *The Psychoanalytic Review*, 66 (1979): 407–422; Dennis Klein, "*Yonadab* : Peter Shaffer's Earlier Dramas Revisited," p. 77, note 8.

17. Janine Chasseguet-Smirgel, *Creativity and Perversion* (London: W. W. Norton and Company, 1985), pp. 3–4. I wish to thank Professor Betsy Draine for calling this work to my attention.

18. Ibid., p. 13.

19. The point is made in both versions of the drama, though perhaps it is most striking in the first unpublished version: "You have entered in fact into Yonadab's world, my friends—watching experience as a dog watches a newspaper; seeing the *signs* for things: perpetually illiterate" (*Yonadab* 1985, I, ix).

20. Yonadab thus reasserts Dysart's revolt in *Equus* against mainstream theology as the only acceptable category for religious experience and the "Normal" as the only acceptable category for sex.

21. Claude Lévi-Strauss, *Structural Anthropology* (Garden City, N.Y.: Anchor Books, 1967), p. 212.

22. Peter Shaffer, *Equus* in *The Collected Plays of Peter Shaffer* (New York: Harmony Books, 1982), p. 448.

23. "Thus the part played by the oceanic feeling, which might seek something like the restoration of limitless narcissism, is ousted from a place in the foreground. The origin of the religious attitude can be traced back in clear outlines as far as the feeling of infantile helplessness. There may be something further behind that, but for the present it is wrapped in obscurity"—Sigmund Freud, *Civilization and Its Discontents*, trans. James Strachey (New York: W. W. Norton and Company, 1961), p. 19.

24. Friedrich Nietzsche, *The Birth of Tragedy*, trans. Walter Kaufmann (New York: Vintage Books, 1967), p. 37.

25. Cooke and Page, *File on Shaffer*, p. 74.

26. C. J. Gianakaris, "Placing Shaffer's *Lettice and Lovage* in Perspective," *Comparative Drama*, 22 (1988): 148.

27. Ibid., p. 150. Frank Rich, reviewing the New York production in the *New York Times*, makes a similar observation but takes a less appreciative view: "*Lettice and Lovage* is essentially a high camp, female version of the archetypal Shaffer play, most recently exemplified by *Equus* and *Amadeus*, in which two men, one representing creativity and ecstatic passion and the other mediocrity and sterility, battle for dominance"— Rich, "Maggie Smith, the One and Many, in *Lettice*," *New York Times*, 26 March 1990, Sec. B, p. 1.

28. Peter Shaffer, *Lettice and Lovage* (New York: Harper and Row, 1990), I, ii, p. 25. Subsequent references are cited parenthetically in the text.

29. Adrienne Rich has suggested that it would be useful to extend the definition of a lesbian relationship beyond the clinical confines of genital experience "to embrace many more forms of primary intensity between and among women, including the sharing of a rich inner life"—a description that might be applied to Lettice and Lotte's relationship. See Adrienne Rich, "Compulsory Heterosexuality," *The Signs Reader: Women, Gender, & Scholarship*, ed. Elizabeth Abel and Emily K. Abel (Chicago: University of Chicago Press, 1983), pp. 156–157.

30. William Butler Yeats, *Collected Poems* (New York: Macmillan, 1956), p. 336.

# CONTRIBUTORS

**C. J. Gianakaris**, a professor of English and Theatre at Western Michigan University, has published widely on Peter Shaffer, including a new book *Peter Shaffer* with Macmillan in London.

**Michael Hinden** is Professor of English at the University of Wisconsin-Madison who often publishes on Shaffer and Eugene O'Neill.

**Dennis A. Klein**, Professor of Modern Languages at the University of South Dakota, has written extensively on Peter Shaffer, including his *Peter Shaffer* in Twayne's British dramatists series.

**Felicia Londré** is Curators' Professor of Theatre at the University of Missouri-Kansas City. Her interests in drama and theater of all eras have led to books on Stoppard, Lorca, Williams, and Shakespeare.

**Barbara Lounsberry** is Professor of English at Northern Iowa University. She has published numerous studies on Shaffer and other modern dramatists.

**Charles R. Lyons**, Margery Bailey Professor of English and Dramatic Literature at Stranford University, has written widely on drama, including books on Shakespeare, Ibsen, Beckett, and Brecht.

**Gene A. Plunka** teaches English at Memphis State University and has published *Peter Shaffer: Roles, Rites, and Rituals in the Theater* with the Fairleigh Dickinson University Press in 1988.

**James R. Stacy** originally wrote the essay included here for *Educational Theatre Journal* in 1976.

# PLAY OPENINGS

"The Salt Land" (television drama—unpublished), 8 Nov. 1955—ITV, London

"The Prodigal Father" (radio drama—unpublished), 14 Sept. 1957— BBC Radio

"Balance of Terror" (television play—unpublished), 21 Nov, 1957— BBC Television; 27 Jan. 1958—CBS Television, New York

*Five Finger Exercise*, 16 July 1958—Comedy Theatre, London; 2 Dec. 1959—Music Box Theater, New York

*The Private Ear* (presented with *The Public Eye*), 10 May 1962—Globe Theatre, London; 9 Oct. 1963—Morosco Theatre, New York

*The Public Eye* (presented with *The Private Ear*), 10 May 1962—Globe Theatre, London; 9 Oct. 1963—Morosco Theatre, New York

"The Merry Roosters Panto" (holiday mime entertainment), 17 Dec. 1963—Wyndham's Theatre, London

*The Royal Hunt of the Sun,* 7 July 1964—National Theatre at Chichester, later at Old Vic Theatre, London; 26 Oct. 1965— ANTA Theatre, New York

*Black Comedy* 27 July 1965—National Theatre at Chichester, later at Old Vic Theatre, London; 12 Feb. 1967—Ethel Barrymore Theatre, New York (with *White Lies*)

*White Lies* (presented with *Black Comedy*), 12 Feb. 1967—Ethel Barrymore Theatre, New York; 21 Feb. 1968—Lyric Theatre, London (revised as *The White Liars*)

*The Battle of Shrivings* (revised as *Shrivings*, 1974), 5 Feb. 1970— Lyric Theatre, London

*Equus*, 26 July 1973—National Theatre, at the Old Vic Theatre, London; 24 Oct. 1974—Plymouth Theatre, New York

*Amadeus*, 2 Nov. 1979—National Theatre, London; 17 Dec. 1980— Broadhurst Theatre, New York

*Yonadab*, 4 Dec. 1985—National Theatre, London

*Lettice and Lovage*, 27 Oct. 1987—Globe Theatre, London; 25 Mar.
   1990—Ethel Barrymore Theatre, New York (revised as *Lettice &*
   *Lovage*)
"Whom Do I Have the Honour of Addressing?"—(radio play), May
   1989—BBC Radio

# SELECTED BIBLIOGRAPHY

## I. Texts of Published Plays

All of Peter Shaffer's earlier published plays are available in: *The Collected Plays of Peter Shaffer* (New York: Harmony Books, 1982). This volume also includes an extensive introductory commentary by the playwright. Shaffer's more recent plays can be found in: Peter Shaffer, *Lettice and Lovage* and *Yonadab* (London: Penguin, 1989).

Shaffer's most recent work, the radio drama "Whom Do I Have the Honour of Addressing?" (1989), is scheduled for publication by André Deutsch, London.

## II. Full Treatments of Shaffer's Drama

*File on Shaffer*, compiled by Virginia Cooke and Malcolm Page. London: Methuen, 1987.

Gianakaris, C. J. *Peter Shaffer*. Macmillan Modern Dramatists Series. London: Macmillan, 1991.

Klein, Dennis A. *Peter Shaffer*. Twayne English Authors. Boston, Mass.: G. K. Hall, 1979.

Plunka, Gene A. *Peter Shaffer [:] Roles, Rites, and Rituals in the Theater*. Rutherford, N.J.: Fairleigh Dickinson Univ. Press, 1988.

Taylor, John Russell. *Peter Shaffer*. Writers and Their Work Series. London: Longman, 1974.

## III. Essays on Shaffer's Works

Buckley, Tom. "'Write Me,' Said the Play to Peter Shaffer." *New York Times Magazine,* 13 Apr. 1975, p. 20 ff.

Dean, Joan F. "Peter Shaffer's Recurrent Character Type." *Modern Drama,* 21 (Sept. 1978), 297–306.

Ebner, Dean. "The Double Crisis of Sexuality and Worship in Shaffer's *Equus*." *Christianity and Literature*, 31 (1982): 29–47.

Gianakaris, C. J. "A Playwright Looks at Mozart: Peter Shaffer's *Amadeus*." *Comparative Drama*, 15 (Spring 1981): 37–53.

———. "Drama into Film: the Shaffer Situation." *Modern Drama*, 28 (Mar. 1985): 83–98.

———. "*Lettice & Lovage:* Fountainhead of Delight." *Theater Week* (2 Apr. 1990): 22–25.

———. "Shaffer's Revisions in *Amadeus*." *Theatre Journal*, 25 (1983): 88–101.

Gelatt, Roland. "Peter Shaffer's *Amadeus:* a Controversial Hit." *Saturday Review*, Nov. 1980, pp. 11–14.

Glenn, Jules. "Alan Strang as an Adolescent: a Discussion of Peter Shaffer's *Equus*." *International Journal of Psychoanalytic Psychotherapy*, 5 (1976): 473–487.

———. "Twins in Disguise: A Psychoanalytic Essay on *Sleuth* and *The Royal Hunt of the Sun*." *Psychoanalytic Quarterly*, 43 (1974): 288–302.

Hinden, Michael. "Trying to Like Shaffer." *Comparative Drama*. 19 (Spring 1985): 14–29.

Huber, Warner, and Hubert Zapf. "On the Structure of Peter Shaffer's *Amadeus*." *Modern Drama*, 28 (1984): 299–313.

Klein, Dennis A. "*Amadeus:* the Third Part of Peter Shaffer's Dramatic Trilogy." *Modern Languages Studies*, 13 (1983): 31–38.

Lounsberry, Barbara. "God-Hunting: the Chaos of Worship in Peter Shaffer's *Equus* and *The Royal Hunt of the Sun*." *Modern Drama*, 21 (1978): 13–28.

Morley, Sheridan. "Cheers for Maggie Smith." *Playbill*, 30 June 1990, pp. 8, 10, 12.

Plunka, Gene A. "The Existential Ritual: Peter Shaffer's *Equus*." *Kansas Quarterly*, 12 (Fall 1980): 87–97.

Walls, Doyle W. "*Equus:* Shaffer, Nietzsche, and the Neuroses of Health." *Modern Drama*. 27 (1984): 314–323.

# INDEX

*177*